— LEGACY —

THE
PROMISED LAND

BOOK ONE

ROSE MARIE HARPER

— LEGACY —

THE
PROMISED LAND

Book One

ROSE MARIE HARPER

Published By:
Brentwood Christian Press
4000 Beallwood Avenue
Columbus, Georgia 31904

Introduction

"Only take heed to thyself, and keep thy soul diligent, less thou forget the things which thine eyes have seen, and less they depart from thy heart all the days of thy life: *but teach them thy sons, and thy sons' sons." -Deut. 4:9*

"And thou shalt teach them diligently unto thy children, and shalt talk of them when thou sittest in thine house, and when thou walkest by the way, and when thou liest down, and when thou riseth up. And thou shalt bind them for a sign upon thine hand, and they shalt be as frontlets between thine eyes. And thou shalt write them upon the posts of thy house and on thy gates."   -Deut. 6:7-9

"Praise ye the Lord. Blessed is the man that feareth the Lord, that delighteth greatly in his commandments. *His seed shall be mighty upon earth:* the generation of the upright shall be blessed…his horn shall be exalted with honor."   -Psalm 112:1-3, 9

I present to you a saga. It is a saga of generations. We "stand on the shoulders of giants." We stand on the shoulders of bygone men, women, and children, ordinary people, like you and me. Yet they were extraordinary. For because of them, we are what we are. When I read the scripture, "His seed shall be mighty upon earth," I wonder. Are we as 'mighty' as we should be? Have we lived up to the example of the score of people who have walked this path before us?

Generations ago, the Harper Family did not belong to royalty, although history shows that at one time 'harpers' were members of the royal courts. Though 'non-royal', they were special. They were special in the sense that they were among the pioneers who brought greatness to the United States of America. They loved each other. They had strong family values. They worked hard and sacrificed daily. But most importantly, they loved and served God. What a heritage for us!

A Note From the Author

This book is historical fiction. A portion of the data concerning the Harpers is factual, denoted by an asterisk (*). The footnotes at the end of Book I indicate the sources of the factual material, collected from the writings or notes of bona fide researchers of the "Harper Lineage."

This is the Harpers' LEGACY. As readers, perhaps you have similar ones. Enjoy!

"Like leaves in trees, the race of man is found, new green in youth, now withering in the ground; another race the following spring supplies. They rise, and then, successive lies: so generations in their course decay, so flourish these, when those are passed away."

Anonymous

TABLE OF CONTENTS

— LEGACY —

THE
PROMISED LAND

A rigid, lifeless form slid from the railing of the ship into the torpid, green ocean. The weight attached to the foot of the body jerked it quickly under the water. It was gone. Several stood on the deck and watched. Most were too sick to care. The air was still and laden with the smell of death. For two weeks the ship had drifted, days under the burning sun, and nights, hot and breezeless. Before the deadly calm the people on board with cries of desperation had lifted fervent prayers to the Almighty to free them from the storms with its high winds and rough waters the ship had known since departing the port of Bristol, England. But they had not prayed for such drifting. The sails above were limp. Not a speck of air moved. Drifting, drifting, drifting, the ship seemed to pause lifeless in the middle of a vast, unfriendly lake, the treacherous Atlantic Ocean.

The captain of the vessel, Hamilton Elsnor, locked himself in his cabin, anything to assign himself to oblivion, to put out the sight and smell of death rampant in his ship. He knew the problem. He knew what was killing his people, one by one. It was not just the calm of the ocean that kept his craft in a drifting pattern. It was the cholera. He moaned, and wished that he could wipe out the voice of the sea captain he had heard in the port of Bristol. "We suffered death, Mate. Cholera! It was only a matter of days, I tell you!" As Elsnor listened to the man rave, he thought he was quite mad. But now he knew. Cholera had hit his ship, the DILI-GENCE, the finest craft that sailed the Atlantic Ocean.

Captain Hamilton Elsnor of the king's royal navy recorded in his log, "I am convinced that this damnable, insufferable heat, together with the constant dampness has brought this plague upon my ship. I know when the plague began. It began on the thirty-eighth day at sea when First Mate Egars became violently ill. Perhaps he was a carrier. I shall never know. When he passed from this world, his body was on fire, and had turned a devilish blue, almost purple. The course of the disease was perplexing to me and the ship's doctor. At first he fainted from weakness, and then began uncontrollable vomiting, followed by rampant diarrhea. The skin on his face and arms sagged like rubber. Each day his eyes sank further into his face as he screamed for water. Toward the end, his voice was a whisper, but all could hear, "The pain. The pain!"

His journal continued, "We have just committed his body to the eternal deep. God rest his soul." Unbeknown to the captain, before the voyage finished, fifteen more of his crew would contract cholera, and dozens of his passengers would die from the dreaded disease.

It was the first time the DILIGENCE had carried human cargo to the new land. The thought of such from the beginning had filled Hamilton Elsnor with dread. At first he had stomped his feet and gone into a tirade as he refused to comply with orders from the King himself. But one of his compatriots made him realize the magnitude of resisting royal orders. "If the King's men come and get ya, ya do as you're told, and if you don't, they hang ya from the nearest yardarm! Then where will you be? Dead, Mate, dead! It's not like it was in old times, Hamilton, when ya owned your own ship."

In time Elsnor submitted to the will of King George, who was bound and determined to rid England of every existing Quaker that ever graced the shores of the motherland. The DILIGENCE was commissioned by royal edict to transport one hundred and fifty Quakers from Bristol England to America, the destination Philadelphia. Begrudgingly, Elsnor allowed his ship to be used as a human garbage dump, for the sea captain was convinced that many of the hapless Quakers would die a terrible death at sea.

Tired, worn, cold and hungry, the Quakers lined up on the dock awaiting a magical transport to the New World. In order to qualify for departure the emigrants had to have certificates from their diocese, their pastors and priests authorizing their departures. Many of the displaced families roamed the docks for months as they begged and sought permission to board one of the ships bound for America. The pilgrims slept, ate, and camped on the docks, as they guarded their meager belongings. They had no alternative because they had, for the most part, been driven from their homes by the Church of England.

Hamilton Elsnor's childhood reeked of such persecution. The sea captain was full of memories of his past. He remembered his sweet, kind mother fluttering about their small cottage that was nestled in the copse of a green valley about fifty kilometers north of London. His father was stern, serious, and non-forgiving, a formidable image that frightened the small boy most of the time. As a young boy, Elsnor would work hard to finish his many duties and chores around the compound in which he lived, and then he and his best friend, Thomas Mullins, would take to the moors clinging bare-back to their horses, and gallop away, with the winds whistling through their ears, and their long hair streaming down their backs. Yes! How Elsnor could remember.

Elsnor remembered that he and Tommy felt as free as birds after a grueling day of milking, cleaning the barn and slopping the pigs. Their ride was breathtaking as they viewed the purple heather as far as the eye could see.

He remembered that the two of them had happened on a copse of trees around which were tethered fifteen horses. They heard angry voices of men shouting, and as they crept forward to listen, Elsnor was dumbfounded to hear the angry voice of his father. It was a brittle and hard voice, one he couldn't help but recognize. His father was one of a group swathed in black coats with black hoods on their heads. His father was screaming as he shouted, "We will hang them all. Meet in the town square at midnight. They are destroying the church. They blaspheme. They die!" Another shouted, "Death to them, for they want to do away with the church's Book of Common Prayer. Quakers! Puritans! They die!"

The terrified boys hovered in the shadows as the men mounted their horses and galloped away. For a minute neither one of them said a word, Elsnor remembered. But then his best friend, Tommy Mullins, said something to him that was unforgivable, that cut like a knife, something he would never forget. "Your father is a murderer! A killer! A killer!" Tommy jumped on his horse and was gone in a minute. He never saw Tommy again.

Hamilton never forgave him for calling his father a murderer. In fact, he remembered, he was certain that it was all a mistake, that his father could not have been involved in persecuting these poor people. But that night, he heard the bedroom door of his parents' open, and heard his father tromping down the steps, mounting his horse and galloping off in the midnight hours. The next day it was reported that a family of six, a mother and father, and four children, all Quakers, had been hung in the city square. And then, he remembered; he knew it was his father and his supposed friends that had been responsible for this dastardly deed. The very next night, Hamilton gathered a bit of food and a knapsack, and stealthily crept away. He headed for the docks, where he found portage on a ship going to the New World. And there on the ships, and the docks, and the sea, he had grown up. He never went home again.

After spending precious time remembering and contemplating his past, Elsnor shook himself from reverie and proceeded to handle the business at hand. "Watson, get those clowns on the dock, (referring to the King's men) to let those people onboard. We have been delayed far too long. We will be missing the prevailing good winds that are blowing in our favor right now. If we wait too long, all hell will break loose when we hit the open water. If it's a norther', we will be lucky to stay afloat."

His man, Watson, hurried to the dock to try to facilitate matters. But nothing seemed to hurry the king's pompous men. Days went by before the DILIGENCE broke anchor and headed out to open sea.

Elsnor watched his new cargo board his ship for a new world and what they hoped was a new beginning. He knew that for some of them, it was their first sail, and also possibly the final journey of their lives. He watched large families board, from the tiniest infant to the gray-haired grandparents.

Yes, later, as Elsnor sat in his cabin and brooded, he anguished over the unexpected stilling of the winds, and their idling on the waters for days after days, and soon weeks after weeks. Somehow the sea captain would rather handle wind and storms, rather than an ungodly, stifling calm on the waters.

After swigging down the last vestige of whiskey he had on the ship, Elsnor fell into a fitful sleep. He had to find a way to forget and escape death. As he finally passed out in a tortured sleep, he prayed to the Almighty that those entrusted to his care would escape the deadly cholera, and that by chance, even by a faint chance, the winds would blow again so the DILIGENCE could be on its way.

Before dawn the beleaguered captain was awakened by a tremendous thud, and then a rhythmic swaying of his bunk. He shouted for joy. "Wind, wind. We have been given the gift of the wind. Thank God. Thank God!" He threw himself out of his cabin onto the upper deck where in wonderment and thanksgiving, he could see outlined in the coming dawn the billows of the DILIGENCE's sails. The winds were filling the sails as high as the yardarm reached to the sky, and for the first time in weeks, the ship was beginning to move. "Thank God. Thank God," was all Elsnor could whisper under his breath.

Dawn wakened all others who were either confined to the hold, or the one wealthy passenger that had a cabin all of his own. One by one the Quakers poured out of the either the bowels of the ship, while the one private passenger that the DILIGENCE carried did not make his appearance. Hamilton Elsnor was just as glad. He did not look forward to dealing with him. As a whole his cargo was holding up as well as could be expected. Elsnor greeted each one as he emerged from his quarters with a smile and a bow. The passengers soaked in the sunshine, the first they had seen since leaving Bristol, England. Elsnor could see that his passengers relished the opportunity of breathing fresh air. He didn't dare question one of them regarding any that might be ill in the hold. He knew for a fact, however, that more than a few of the emigrants were lying in filth and vomiting, victims of the indescribable horror, cholera.

The sea captain watched his flock with concern and interest. The Quakers were gathered in small groups on the deck. Some chatted while others engaged in what appeared to be fierce debate. He smiled as he perused the women folk, most of whom appeared weak and unable to cope with their situation; however, he knew that the pioneer spirit that burned within the breast of the women was the spark that would keep kith and kin alive on the far-off shore they were hoping to reach. They were the heartbeat of the black-coated, high-hatted gentlemen that crowded the deck.

The peace of the day vanished when Elsnor heard the unmistakable roaring of his one high-paying passenger, who occupied one of the two rentable cabins on the ship. At that point Elsnor's head began to pound. He remembered how this passenger had acted on the dock before they set sail. He appeared on the dock in a magnificent black carriage. As an old country boy, Elsnor at that time couldn't help but admire the stallions that pulled the brougham. The attendant steering the horses reined them to a standstill, and then what Elsnor considered to be fireworks, began. The man that stepped from the carriage had a flowing black cloak. He tipped his high bowler hat as he gave his hand to an elegant lady, clothed in silks and satin. After her, two younger women dismounted the carriage. They appeared to be ladies-in-waiting, for whom Elsnor thought was possibly royalty of some nature or another.

The rude, loud passenger-to-be pulled the whip from the driver's hands, and struck the backs of the beautiful stallions that Elsnor felt so much an identity with. The whip left a huge welt on the back of one of the beasts. The unwelcomed passenger shoved and pushed his way to the gangplank to board the DILIGENCE. He shoved and spit at the poor souls that still had not been able to board any of the ships bound for America, because of one hang up or another.

"Away! Away! Get away! Animals! Animals!" The man cursed the hapless pioneers as he bulldozed his way to the DILIGENCE. Elsnor shuddered as he watched. The unwelcome passenger stumbled as he made his way up the gangplank, and the sea captain had to squelch laughing at the passenger-to-be that looked like such a clumsy idiot. A host of swearing came from his mouth, as he approached closer to the cabin with contempt and malice dripping from his mouth. Elsnor didn't like the man, not one bit. The captain knew he would be a troublemaker from the onset of the voyage.

"You! You!" he shouted. "You must be the captain of this magnificent vessel!" Sarcasm dripped from his mouth. He thrust a sheaf of papers into Elsnor's hands.

"I am Tremaine Devore, commissioned by his Majesty King George I!" He looked around in disgust. "Unfortunately I have been ordered by the king to apprise this vessel and command it until it reaches port in Philadelphia." While he bellowed, his stained, yellow teeth protruded from his lips. Immediately Elsnor took offense.

The interloper continued. "Now that this hulk of a ship has been seized by His Royal Highness, he wishes to know that it is seaworthy. The king will have no old wreck as part of his royal navy." Elsnor backed away. It was the first time he had heard that the king considered his personal pride and joy, the DILIGENCE, to be part and parcel of his royal navy. Just thinking about the possibility made the gracious sea captain steam with anger.

Devore went on, "I have been ordered to approve of the passengers on this ship. I can see right away you are not accepting enough of those dirty Quakers in the hold. The king is most anxious to rid his kingdom of all of those disgusting people. I plan to watch these passengers with the reputation of the king solidly in mind. And if they should act badly and blemish the reputation of the king, they will be hanged. I will see to it." Elsnor blanched in anger and disgust. "And oh yes, my distinguished career on the sea should help you navigate this heap over the ocean to America." His fat chest puffed out with pride.

A diminutive woman appeared by his side. It was his wife. She looked frightened and ill at ease. "Now," he purred like a wildcat waiting to spring, "if you will show us to our cabin, we shall get unpacked and hopefully be on our way!" He looked over the crew and commented, "Motley crew! Motley! And to think that I could be sipping tea at Lady Hawthorne's estate. Disgusting! Disgusting!" He turned to give orders to his pale, frightened wife. "Tabitha! Tabith! On with you now, we must get settled. I'll not have you standing around with the crew gawking at you. Move!"

Following his tirade, Devore spit on the clean, polished deck of the DILIGENCE, an act never tolerated by the sea captain before. Elsnor bit his tongue, and let the unwelcome pair descend to their cabin in the front of the ship. He wondered if Devore wouldn't be the one facet of his entire trip that might cause the DILIGENCE to flounder halfway between England and the new world.

Later that day Elsnor relaxed and once again felt himself swaying to the constant rhythms of the waves. He looked at the setting sun and realized it was time to call for the night watchman to take command. But suddenly he realized he had a companion by his side. The captain thought him to be about ten years old. The young lad had a winsome face and a head full of russet, wavy hair. Without speaking he joined the captain and looked out over the water.

"Pretty, eh what, young feller?" The captain didn't wait for an answer but continued to speak, more to himself than the young boy. "The sea'll git in your bones afore you know what happened to ya? Agree?"

The young boy nodded and smiled as he looked up.

"Look over there Son," the captain pointed to the sides of the ship. Schools of large fish ran alongside the vessel. "Them's grampuses. Look over there, them's porpoises, all out there to play with the ship. See 'em?" The captain didn't wait for an answer but hit the boy on the shoulder. "Hey! Young Man. Way out there. See? Them's great whales, great whites I think. Hard to believe they're this far north this time of the year!"

The young man quivered in shared excitement. He too saw a pair of great whales that to his eyes looked like big oxen as they jumped high into the air, all the while spewing water like smoke coming from a chimney. When they dived under water, they left behind a cloud of white foam. "They's as big as oxes!"

"Sure are, Son. That's a real privilege to see those monsters of the deep. Say, my name's Captain Elsnor. What's yours, Son? And by the way, how old are you?"

"Ten, sir. Almost eleven. And, oh yes, my name is Castleton. Castleton Harper, spelt with an 'E,' you know, rather than a 'U.' The royal master put us down with an 'E.'"

"A good name, Lad. And who might you be with?"

"My parents, Sir, my mother and father. Then there's my brother, Josiah, and my baby sister, who was just born a couple of months ago."

"Are you the youngest son?"

"'Fraid I am, sir. The whole family treats me like a very young person, a child you know, but I really am close to being a man. I am going to Philadelphia and be a man, learn a trade and get my own land," he said boastfully.

"Reckon you will, young man. Reckon you will." The captain paused in his conversation, and then continued. "Your ma and your pa, and your brother and sister, are they holding up? How are they faring down there?" He pointed to the hold.

"All right I guess. They was all mighty sick the first week or so with all that rocking of the boat. Not me though, I'm tough, I can take it. I guess they are all right." He paused and then grinned. "I had to come up here for a while, Sir. The stench is pretty bad down there, you know what I mean? And it seems like all of the babies are crying."

"I'm sure young man, that you will be a real man very soon, very soon." The kind sea captain smiled down at the boy.

The boy, anxious to talk, spieled off the saga of his life. "You know they all think I'm a child. But I'm not, Captain," he looked up. "I know what this journey is all about. You see, I can remember a year or so ago when we lost everything to the abbott, that man from that big church. They told us he was the ruler now, called the Church of England. We lived in Derby, you know, with a farm and all that sort of thing. It was nice," he looked out over the water as he wistfully remembered. "We had horses and pigs, a couple of servants and a nice house. But one day when my father got home from the meeting house where our church met, that mean old abbott from that big church was there with some of the king's troops. He told my father that we had to leave right away and go, that our land and house belonged to him and not my father. If we didn't go, my father was going to be whipped and put in jail. My mother hid in the kitchen. She was crying all the time. I was scared to death, so I hid in one of the bushes, 'cause I thought they might take me to jail or something. Josiah grabbed a stick and started to hit the abbott and beat on his horse. But my father stopped him. I can remember him saying, 'Son, Quakers do not fight, ever!'

"At any rate, early the next morning we left our house. We tried to pile everything on a cart, but stuff kept falling off. When we all climbed aboard, my grandparents wouldn't come, Captain. They said they would find a place to stay in the village. They said they were too old to leave it all behind. I guess I understand," the child reflected. "But I miss them. I still do." A tear started down his cheek, but he quickly brushed it off. "Well, we finally made it to Leicester where we decided to stay. We lived in a little flat that had an upstairs and a small downstairs. We were there until the day after some of my relatives came in by horseback from Derby. That's when we left. The night before I knew something big was going on. Everybody had a fearful look on their faces, especially the men-folk. I can remember that night they talked for a long time. Father made me go to bed upstairs, and Mother came up too since she had to nurse my baby sister. Josiah got to stay with the men-folk while they talked. They all thought he was old enough, so he stayed downstairs. Even though they made me leave, Captain, I heard it all. They thought I wasn't listening, but I was. I heard everything. There was talk about something called a purge. Our meeting house in Derby had been burned, and a couple of the men my father knew had been thrown into prison. Everything happening back in Derby sounded awful. They said this purge, whatever that is, was going to start in Leicester, and that no Quaker would be safe. I don't know why, but everyone seemed to hate our church. Bad. Our relatives told Father that we must leave, or he would be arrested, especially since he had been a spokesman at the meeting house. I think my father was scared. I know I was. Then my father and the men prayed. And after the prayer, my father didn't seem to be afraid anymore. He told the others how several days before he had received a letter from my Uncle John, who was one of the first to go over with a Mr. Penn to a place they call Philadelphia. Anyhow, Uncle John had a lot of land a little away from this Philadelphia, a place he called Oxford, like the town in England, you know? Uncle John wrote that he wanted our family to come to Oxford to live with him. Captain, it was real quiet downstairs for a long time after that. Nobody said anything. Then Father spoke. He said the letter was a divine message. It was a message from God. And that we would go.

"After our friends left the next morning, Father told Mother we were going to the new world and to get everything packed up again. She cried. She did not want to come, Captain Elsnor. I think she worried about baby sister, being as how she is so little, you know. Anyhow, Captain, here we are. We are going to see Uncle John. He surely will be surprised when we show up. It will be neat, Captain. Uncle John wrote about all the good things that were happening, all the opportunities and stuff. We are going to ride out and meet Uncle John as soon as we can get a horse and some things together. It's kind of exciting, don't you think, Captain?"

"Aye, Lad. That it is. That it is."

"Be kind of nice to go to church when we want and where we want and not have to worry about getting hurt, or run out, or something like that. Yes, Sir. I just know Philadelphia is the place to go, then we can go out from there." He looked up. And then questioning, "We going to get there soon, Captain? Soon?"

"Won't be too much longer, Lad, not too much longer. Now you best get down to your folks. They will be looking for you." The young man seemed satisfied with all that he had told the captain, and with the captain's response. With a brief farewell he hastened away to his place in the hold.

The ship had lost sight of all land on the thirteenth day at sea. As the DILIGENCE left the Bristol harbor, it was accompanied by three other vessels, the captains of which hoped to make the journey together. Captain Elsnor was particularly hopeful that HMS, the JAMES, would stay with the DILIGENCE. The JAMES, a frigate of 300 tons, also was carrying a group of Quakers to Philadelphia. In addition, the vessel, the BESS, and the ANGEL GABRIEL were bound for Massachusetts and the New England area with a load of Puritans. There had been a lot of bad feeling between the Quakers and the Puritans on the dock. The captain was happy to get his passengers loaded so that the confrontation, which seemed about to explode before departure between the sects, would come to an end.

As soon as the ships cleared Bristol Bay, rough waters had begun to swell and beat against the vessel. Periodically the captain could hear the moaning and the groaning of his passengers in the hold. They had become deathly sick from the violent pitching of the ship. He wished that he could calm the sea, but his wishes and even his prayers were to no avail. Finally, however, on the morning of the thirteenth day, dawn had come over a sea that rippled and for the most drifted quietly. A thick, dense fog enveloped the DILIGENCE like a glove, and the watch on the mast could see nothing. Vainly the DILIGENCE searched the horizon for sight of its fellow ship, the JAMES. The JAMES had vanished. The DILIGENCE was alone.

In his dreams the captain relived the days that followed. They were good days. There was usually a fine gale of wind north and east that filled the sails and kept the vessel scudding across the water. Often there were sudden showers of mist, rain or snow, and always the heavy spray driven by the wind. He had written in his log, "On day 25, the crew deems that we are near some land because the color of the water has changed. They dropped a sounding line 160 fathom but could reach no bottom. As much as I wished that we were near the shore, I realized we were still far distant. I scoffed at the excitement of the men. Still, they replied with jocularity. The feelings aboard are good, and the passengers and crew seemingly in good spirits."

The next day, "The winds have become very cold as if it might be December. There is approaching, however, a good gale of southerly winds which allow the ship seven leagues a watch. With the changing winds, the wind has become stronger and a rough night has prevailed. Passengers are complaining of the dampness and the leaking of the water through the sides of the ship."

The next day, "We have experienced a great calm. It is very hot. Our people are much afflicted with fainting, sweating and heat. A little land bird with blue-colored feathers about the bigness of a sparrow landed on our ship. Then a mighty gale proceeded from the south, which though weak and soft did not mitigate the head."

In his mind the captain could clearly see the dawning of the third day of the calm when a stalwart-looking, tall gentleman came up from the hold and approached him. He looked very much like his new young friend, Castleton, who the captain had not seen for some days.

"Captain," as he extended his hand, "My name is Harper, Castleton Harper. It is a pleasure to meet thee. I am sorry that it has taken so long for me to approach thou. But I have been very busy tending to my wife and family below."

Surprised that he was now meeting the second Castleton, the captain replied. "Oh yes, Mr. Harper. I have met your youngest son, Castleton, also, I believe. Is he well? I have missed seeing him."

"Yes, he is quite well. He has had to stay below quite a bit and help tend to his young sister and his mother. She has not been very well. But as soon as we land, I am quite sure she will revive. And when might that be, Captain?"

"It is hard to know, Sir. In this calm we are more or less at a complete standstill. It is only in the hands of the Almighty when the DILIGENCE shall move."

The two men struck up a friendly conversation, and before long the elder Castleton Harper held the captain in rapt attention as he described his vision of the new Pennsylvania.

"You know, Captain, William Penn was the greatest visionary of our church. He had a driving energy to find a land for us without war, where the poorest man could live in peace and support himself in decency. He became a Friend and received the inner light in Ireland, you know, one evening in Cork. He just happened into a meeting. He was a member of the King's advisors and quite high up in the court of the King. But he became aware of an inner light glowing within our people. He earnestly prayed and sought this inner light. And as I have been told, with tears rolling down his cheeks, he became a Quaker and accepted our cause. He is a brave man, Captain.

The captain recalled that the face of the elder Castleton Harper was glowing as he raved about William Penn. "Yes, Captain, my family and I are going to Pennsylvania for freedom, to worship as we please. I have a commitment to a shipping firm on the dock for work for a short time, and then my family and I will be joining my brother, John. He has a settlement a short distance from Philadelphia that he says is quite nice with a lot of opportunities for craftsmen and the like with good wages." Castleton, Sr., laughed a hearty laugh. "It all promises to be a blessing to me and my family. We worship a good and gracious God, Captain. A good and gracious God!"

He had little more to say, but bid the captain farewell as he returned to his family, but not before he remarked about the oppressive heat and the fact that many of his friends bunking in the hold were feeling a peculiar type of malaise. Little did the captain realize at the time that the scourge on his ship had begun.

As his passenger retreated to the hold, the captain recalled thinking as he replied, "Yes, my good, Quaker friend. Please I beg you, pray that Almighty God will cause the breezes to blow!"

The captain dreamed of all these things. But his dreams ended as quickly as they had begun. As dawn burst into the cabin, already the heat was stifling. Elsnor rolled out of his bunk, his head and neck throbbing from all the visions and nightmares of the darkness of the night before. Somehow during his sleep he had hoped that the dawn would bring good fortune, good weather, and good health to his fellow sea-goers. His hopes were dashed immediately. It didn't take too long to realize that he had more death and despair to face during the oncoming days of the DILIGENCE on the waters of the great Atlantic Ocean as the ship wallowed in the great calm.

Getting up, as the captain threw a handful of water on his face, he staggered when he heard a tremendous boom. Thinking a cannon had accidentally discharged, he threw himself from his cabin, but stopped in his tracks. Smoke was billowing from the cabin his hated passenger, Tremaine Devore, shared with his wife. He flung open its door and saw the tiny woman staring, holding a smoking pistol which she had unloaded into Devore's belly. Blood was everywhere. Devore's glassy eyes darted about in absolute amazement, he shouted an obscenity, and then dropped down dead. The Captain was stupefied. As much as he disliked Tremaine Devore, his incessant harrassment of him, his crew, and his pathetic wife, he never in his mind thought he would come to such an end. Mumbling, his hysterical wife muttered, "He hit me, so hard. Now he won't, not ever again." The captain ushered her out of the bloody mess into a cabin held by her maids, dragged Devore up to the deck, and unceremoniously had his crew throw him into the deep. Mrs. Tremaine Devore finished her journey to Philadelphia on the DILIGENCE. After that frightful morning the incident was never metioned again.

On the thirty-ninth day of the voyage, he later recorded in the ship's log, the captain was convinced that the Almighty had answered his prayer. The winds began to blow, and the ship slowly moved out of the devastating calm. In the days and weeks prior forty-six bodies of men, women and children had been committed to the fetid, green waters of the ocean's great calm. He wrote in the ship's log, "On this a Saturday morning, a cool wind at north transpired and our seamen sounded ground at 60 fathom. Another bird from the land came and lit upon the sails of the ship. The calm is over. The winds are again blowing. Praise the Almighty God! The men are now fishing and hauling in cod onto the ship as fast as they can haul them up. Now the diet of the passengers will improve, and with Almighty God's cooling breeze perhaps the scourge soon will be removed. Surely God is delivering us."

His joy was short-lived. Suddenly a great storm caused the few remaining crew members to let down all of the sails. The ship was tossed with feather mountains and valleys of water. The captain was convinced that THE DILIGENCE might be swallowed up. It took all of his strength to man the rudder and keep the ship on an even keel. A form of a rather tall, young man dashed up beside him. The captain was outraged. "Get below, young man," he ordered above the deafening winds. "You will be swept overboard before you can count to ten. Down, I say, go down!"

"Captain," he screamed over the winds. "My brother, Castleton, wants you to come, to come now, below! It's my baby sister. She doesn't move! And my mother, we cannot get her to respond. Come, captain. Castleton said you could help him." He pulled on the slicker of the captain that was coated with the sea's foamy spray.

Grudgingly the captain staggered over to the opening of the hold. He had made it a rule of thumb never to go down into it to see the plight of the people he was carrying. He had had to assist in consigning too many of them to the deep to venture into the hell-pit he knew to be below. But he could in his mind almost see the imploring eyes of the young Castleton, who had reminded him so much of his own son back on the green shores of Ireland. He could not refuse.

The pitching of the ship, and the green mildew that covered the steps down into the hold almost caused the captain to fall head-first. Catching himself and regaining his composure, he took a deep breath and stepped into what to him was a scene from hell. Men, women and children were lying in heaps in scattered areas throughout the skeleton of the ship. The stench was unbearable. Those who were well were vainly trying to spoon gruel into the mouths of the ill. He wanted to retch as he smelled and viewed the abject despair of the scene before him.

As they haltingly made their way into a darkened recess of the ship's bowels, the young man finally spoke. "I'm Josiah, Castleton's brother."

Josiah led him to a prostrate form lying on a makeshift bed made of heavy planks. To one side stood an older man that the captain recognized as the young Castleton's father. In the brief time lapse since their conversation on the deck, the man's face had changed markedly. It had become hollow, pale, and gaunt. He was suffering, that the captain knew for certain.

The young Castleton was sitting on the foot of the board. He held the unseeing, unblinking head of his mother in his arms. He was stroking her hair and patting her face. The woman did not move. In her arms was swaddled an inert form. The captain knew immediately that it was a child, and that the child was dead.

The young Castleton was the first to speak. "Captain Elsnor, I wanted you to come. It's my mother, captain. She will not move or speak. I told father that you would know what to do."

The captain leaned over the form of the lifeless woman. Tenderly he raised her hand to see if he could find the pulse of life in her. There was none. She was dead.

He reached over and gently closed her eyelids.

"I'm sorry." He looked over at the young men and their father. "She is no longer here. She has gone home to be with the Lord."

With that the older man, the father, began to sob. "She did not want to come. She did not believe the church would be purged, that we would suffer. Frightened she was to bring the young, wee child. What have I done to submit her to such a death? What have I done?" With that he began to rock and weep uncontrollably.

The captain was at a loss as to what should transpire next. He did know, however, that the bodies would have to be assigned to the ocean. Gently he removed the dead infant from her arms. As he parted the covers, he knew that cholera had devastated the young, helpless child.

But as he looked at the young mother, he knew that the woman had not died of cholera. Her face was still comely and full. She had not deteriorated. It puzzled him that she had expired. He had no explanation.

He quietly directed the boys to carry the inert forms of their mother and sister to the deck. "Why? Why?" they uttered. The only explanation to the captain was that she had died of shock and dismay. Why else would someone evidently healthy depart to the eternal realm? To himself, the captain reasoned that such had been the cause.

The husband was beyond reason. Alternately he praised and cursed the God that had allowed such a tragedy to befall his family, particularly his beloved wife. He had to be held up as one of

23

the sons assisted him to the deck where the two boys had carried their mother and sister. He wailed and protested the burial of his wife and child in the waters of the sea. But it had to be.

Saying a few words and muttering a brief prayer, the captain gave the signal and one of the crew lowered the two and dropped them into the water as had been done numerous times before. As the bodies disappeared, the elder Castleton Harper began shrieking and shouting to God, "You have forsaken me! You have forsaken me!" And with that he threw himself over the railing of the ship into its tumbling wake. He struggled momentarily as he fell into the water and thrashed wildly around in the sea, but in seconds his body disappeared from view and was gone.

In horror, anguish, and disbelief, Castleton, Jr., and Josiah watched all of this transpire. Within seconds they had become orphaned, without parents, without a sister, completely alone in the world.

The captain felt personally responsible. He grieved as he thought about what had happened to this godly family. Shepherding the boys into the arms of several of the Harpers' friends gathered on the deck to watch the burial, he couldn't bring himself to face the boys, but hurried away to the recesses of his cabin to regain his composure and resilient spirit. He knew he still had to deal with the fate of the rest of the suffering souls on his ship. The death of a certain twosome could not and must not take him from his responsibility. He could not let it! As he slammed the door of his cabin shut, he remembered he had forgotten to be grateful for what had been a temporary spate of the wind. He marveled that the ship had been given a brief respite from all the pitching and tossing, while the captain had proceeded with this, another burial at sea.

As the days progressed, he could not shake his feeling of personal responsibility for the Harper youths, Castleton and Josiah. He could not let them die in the hold. Finally, he made a decision. They would be moved from the hold and transferred to the crews' quarters. The accommodations were not much better, but somewhat. Besides the crew was given better rations and food than those in the hold. Gruffly, as he tried to hide his emotions, he told Josiah and Castleton that they would be moved. Still in shock, they complied in meek obeisance. Gathering up their sparse gear, namely the packs that belonged to their father and mother, the stunned, and momentarily helpless, young men were transferred to the crews' quarters. There they were accepted and given the attention they needed to keep them from dwelling on the tragedy of the recent days. And in the log was posted, "The Harper brothers have been transferred to the crews' quarters. They will receive equal rations and given the attention they deserve. I too, will be able to keep a closer watch on them."

Seventy-five days from Bristol the seamen sighted land. The captain, the crew, and the passengers that were still living, lifted praises to God for assuaging the seas sufficiently to allow them deliverance. But deliverance was not quite theirs, as yet.

As the DILIGENCE floated on the coast, there was a great fog and mist so that the land was blotted out. The ship began losing ground rather than gaining. There was an abundance of rain. Many islands, the sides of which and beaches of which were littered with giant boulders and rocks, could be seen. The wind continued westward, then again southward. There ensued a great storm of rain and easterly winds which put the ship in danger of capsizing. It seemed impossible but the DILIGENCE within sight of land was now having to fight the worst storm of the journey. The passengers huddled in fear, while the seamen above braved the winds and the waves to keep the ship as upright as possible. Water was rising in the hold, and leaking in by the buckets. By the dawn of the next day the ship had lost three great anchors and cables by the violence of the waves. Two were broken by the impact of the crashing water, and the other was cut by a seaman as he tried to save the floundering ship.

God did appear, however. The sails were furled as the wind blew the battered vessel past the rocks, into the harbor and away from the savage sea. The incredible journey had ended. The port of Philadelphia lay beckoning in a dawning sunrise. For the hapless pioneers, the Quakers, now numbering only 65 of the former 150 souls who left Bristol, the journey of their lives was over. They had traveled a thousand leagues or three thousand miles over one of the greatest seas of the world. Only thirteen of Captain Hamilton Elsnor's crew of thirty men survived.

PHILADELPHIA

The DILIGENCE sailed into Delaware Bay on August 16, 1722, after 78 days at sea. The winds, gentle and soft, were a welcome surcease from the havoc that they wrought out in the open sea. Everyone on the vessel seemed to come alive as they hugged the rails of the ship as it made it way up the long Delaware River. As Captain Elsnor apprised the condition of his vessel, his description of "sailing" up the river was probably "limping" up the river. His beloved ship was like a wounded animal. It had almost been torn apart by the storms, and the interior of the ship was so rank and foul that it would require a massive cleanup program to make it fit to ever use for cargo again. He prayed that he would never have to undergo such an ordeal with his beloved DILIGENCE again. He knew it would take weeks and perhaps months of labor to revamp it so that it would once again be seaworthy to make a return voyage to England. But thank God for deliverance! They were at their destination. Finally the DILIGENCE would deliver its passengers. Captain Elsnor would miss them, especially the Harper brothers. He wondered what would become of them. Castleton had proudly informed him that he was now eleven years old; he had been told that Josiah was sixteen. As young men, they both believed they were ready to conquer the new world. The captain sincerely hoped they would not be disappointed in their aspirations.

Suddenly they were within view of the port of Philadelphia. En masse the passengers and crew on board the DILIGENCE let up a cheering shout of thanksgiving for making it to their destination. What they saw ahead was awesome, particularly after their days, weeks and months of travail on the ocean. On the land there was a hubbub of activity. Ships that had come from all over the world lay anchored at the docks. Captain Elsnor hailed the captain of the JAMES from afar. He wondered how its passengers had fared. He mused to himself that they must have found a quicker and faster passage than the DILIGENCE. It was good to see a sister ship.

One could see from the deck of the vessel that the great city business area seemed to be spread out on a vast plain. As one looked farther to the east the city seemed to rise into high foothills, well above the Delaware River. The boys would soon discover that even to the north and northwest the land became elevated and the tall hills covered with thick, immense, dark woods. The city, founded by William Penn as his "Holy Experiment," at first had attracted Welsh Quakers who came over with their wives, children, and servants in 1682. It had boomed and by the 1700s's boasted a population of almost 30,000. German Mennonites, German Moravaians, Scotch-Irish Presbyterians, and even Negro slaves, together with thousands of Quakers who walked the streets of the bustling town, or so the captain explained to the Harper brothers. To the newcomers, especially Castleton and Josiah Harper, the town looked captivating. But the wise, old sea captain knew that indeed, naïve travelers such as the brothers could become entrapped in a kind of trouble from which there was no escape, namely nefarious deals of men and their services, or bootleggers of the flesh. He felt a great need to protect them from all of the untoward influences of the new land that might take advantage of their naiveté.

He herded them along the streets, away from the wharf, and he pushed and shoved them away from scurrilous individuals, poised to take advantage of them. He pumped the boys full of the knowledge that he had. As he walked, Castleton drank in his words of knowledge.

"Men, watch out for all of those wandering around here that are anxious to sell you to the highest bidder. Sort of a slave trade, it is. Castleton, come away from there," he shouted to the young boy as he loitered and looked into one of the dark shops lining the road. "That's a bad place!" The captain clucked to himself, but the boys heard. "Can't understand what's happened around here. You know at the beginning Philadelphia wasn't like this." The captain paused, evidently a bit winded. He was not used to such a brisk pace, much less walking farther than the distance between his ship's railings.

He continued, "William Penn did not conceive of what has befallen Philadelphia today. Of all the English that have received land grants in the new world, William Penn probably had the purest motives in his heart. He did not acquire this land for any personal profit, you understand, not like all of these leeches you see hanging around here trying to steal from you, and do something else bad. No, Penn dreamed of a land and a home for everybody, the lost, the poor, and the down-trodden. He wanted them to make a decent living for their families and go to church wherever they wanted to go. He wanted his new city to be different from England, and particularly different than London, where is where he was born, by the way. Life in London is pretty bad, you know. Too many people live there. They're stacked on each other like wood in a woodpile. And there's no jobs. So people are hungry. They live like dogs, killing and raping each other. I bet you wouldn't want to live like a dog in the street. That's the way it is there, you know? Penn didn't want his new country to be like that. He wanted the houses to be out in the open and separate with plenty of grass and trees between. He said those terrible living conditions caused that big fire in London not long ago. I heard thousands of people got burned up. Penn wanted everything to be beautiful here, with lots of trees and flowers. He wanted everything to be in order too, you know, not helter skelter, not here and there. Order. Beauty. Them's were his bywords. Well, as luck would have it he lived here only two years after he started the place. After that, Penn had to go back to England and settle some kind of a fight he had over there with somebody that said he owed him a lot of money. That was too bad. His 'City of Brotherly Love,' that's what he called it, you know, never was the same after he left. When he lived here, there were about seven hundred houses, I suppose. They were all pretty and laid out like he wanted them to be. I guess the most people counted was forty-five hundred. Gosh, look at this place now. Penn wouldn't and didn't recognize it when he got back. I think there are about thirty thousand here now, and everything is worse than London, just about. He wanted city parks laid out, but as you can see, for the most part, that hasn't happened."*

Truly, the young boys could see that the city had grown like topsy, and that Penn's well-thought-out plans were nowhere to be seen. As they made their way along the wharves, they saw sprawling slums, with bars, rundown housing, and what they found to be whorehouses. Here they learned were places of crime and sickness. The ships brought in diseases from all over the world. Consequently, smallpox epidemics and yellow fever decimated the settlement time after time. They learned that the water supply throughout the city was rank; and that in most of the tenant houses, there was corruption and theft. The Harpers often wondered why folks did not complain to the law enforcement, but they learned that the people received no help. In early Philadelphia no one was in authority or control. Philadelphia's facsimile of government was weak and fraught with corruption. Even in time violent quarreling over taxation of Penn's holdings ensued. They argued over what they considered to be Penn's exorbitant wealth and holdings. In his absence landowners began to complain bitterly about the privileges he enjoyed as Lord Proprietor of Philadelphia. Rather than showing appreciation to their benefactor, many of the new settlers began to rise against Penn and question his integrity and his role as a savior from the ills of their life in England. After a time Penn's vision of the City of Brotherly Love, the Holy Experiment, was forgotten. When the kind gentleman with pure motives and desires returned to his city, he had lost respect and was ruined financially. His dream had ended. And as before, the city continued its haphazard growth.

Into such an environment Captain Hamilton Elsnor shepherded his two young friends along the bustling streets of Philadelphia. He had to get them away to a nicer place, a nicer area in which they could live. He wondered why he felt such a need to do so, to see after their welfare. But as he looked at Castleton, he could see his own son. "Yes," he thought, "I must care for them."

His first order of business was to find them lodging. Urging them ahead as they departed on the gangplank into the bustling activity of the quay, the captain motioned for them to follow. Obediently they followed. They knew not what else to do. They were at a complete loss.

"Lads, I am going to take you up to Lydia Carlsen's boarding house. She's a good woman. I know she will be happy to provide you a room and cook for you for a while." A big grin swept over his swarthy, red-cheeked face. "Yessir, she's a real friend. She'll be happy to take care of you, Men. Come, follow me!"

The two, young boys, guided like lost sheep, felt their panic dissolve. To them nothing sounded better than a nice place to stay, a warm bed, and plenty of good food. Just the thought of leaving that horrid ship almost resulted in them dancing a jig. When Castleton and Josiah saw the confusion and all the hustle and bustle of the new settlement, they were afraid. The captain settled them down. But they were hungry and gazed with wanting at the hawkers that walked the street as they vended rolls, breads, and fruits. The captain did not stop to eat but hurried them on. The trio walked up the streets of the city that rose precipitously from the river.

From Dock Street near the wharves, they walked at least a mile. The streets were long, narrow and straight. Many of them were named after trees. Seedlings of chestnuts, walnut, locust, spruce, and pine were planted in rows along the sides of the streets. Away from the docks the air seemed fresher. Certainly the area became greener, more spacious, and prettier. The captain was pleased about his decision. Anything was better than having his young friends live in the seamy side of the city. He knew that his good friend, Lydia, would welcome the young adventurers with open arms. The young Englishmen walked on with amazement and gasped. They had never seen as much greenery and trees since they had left Derby in what seemed to them to have been eons before. All the sights were so different, especially after seeing nothing but endless ocean. Both of them thanked God for finally having arrived in Philadelphia.

On the western part of town, the boys sighted another river, the Schuylkill. On it they could see many smaller boats, going up and down. "That there river is the Schuylkill, Men. It is much too shallow for large ships," explained the captain. Walking up the hill, the boys could see that the houses were symmetrical and red brick. By the sides of houses were gardens and orchards, and some fields. "Gardens and orchards mean food," the hungry lads salivated. Elsnor was also bone-weary but pleased with the belief that his motherly friend would take the boys in to keep them away from the perilous housing near the city's wharves.

They were very tired, especially young Castleton, as they made their way into the parlor and met the cheery lady, Lydia Carlsen. Scotch-Irish, she greeted them warmly and saw them into a rosy, warm, well-lit room high up in the eaves of her house.

"Young Men, you can stay here as long as you want; this house can be your home. There's a place for you to clean up a bit down at the blockhouse in the back, and you can undo your packs and use the armoire in the corner. Supper'll be in an hour, and I'll call ya's down to eat." She smoothed out her apron and made her way from the room. They could hear her as she went down the wooden steps, "Nothin' I wouldn't do for Hamilton Elsnor. He brung me and my family here, and we owe him our life."

"Cass, I guess you and I are in this together now. Won't be anything that's goin' to separate us." Josiah remarked as he stretched out on one of the two beds. "My, am I glad to be off that ship." His face clouded over in spite of the rays of sun coming through the window. "I will miss Father and Mother, but Father would expect us to go on, you know?"

Castleton nodded. "We will be all right, thanks to the Captain. He has been a real great friend."

"Indeed he has."

"I'm going to go to work, you know. First thing in the morning I am going to get a job."

"Look, Cass. You are probably too young. No one will hire you."

"Maybe the Captain can find a place for me. Maybe." He was quiet for a moment while he thought. "Did Father have any money in his pack, Josiah? Have you looked?"

31

"I haven't wanted to touch any of his things since, well, since the accident, you know?" Josiah hesitated. "But I guess it's time we take a look at everything he had. I think it's all in his pack." And after a moment, "I thought Mother had a pack of things for the baby?"

"No, I don't think so." Castleton answered. "I thought she had her small Testament, but I have not seen it anywhere. Have you?"

Josiah hoisted his father's worn, black backpack on the bed and dumped its contents on the bed. The first thing to fall out was a tattered Bible. Josiah held it in his hands for a moment, thought about it, and finally said, "Cass, I think Father would want us to pray and thank God for our deliverance from the sea. Do you not think so?"

His younger brother nodded, whereupon the two brothers fell to their knees beside the bed and expressed their thanksgiving to God for bringing them safely to the new world. They prayed for a time, and then both of them simultaneously stood up and embraced.

Josiah said, "Don't worry Cass. I will take care of you. Either me, or God." The sixteen-year-old boy did not realize that the first prayers uttered by Castleton and Josiah Harper in the city of Philadelphia were the first to be uttered by a long lineage of Harpers to follow.

They continued to empty the contents of their father's pack. There were a few pieces of clothing, but wrapped in a soft, flannel cloth, two gold pieces tumbled out.

They held the coins reverently. "One will be for you, Cass. The other for me."

"No, Josiah, I can't take one." He said as he handed his coin to his brother. "You will need it to buy clothes, especially if you are going to get a job."

"We will see. We'll see. Really, one of those gold pieces is yours. What's this?"

He held up a worn piece of parchment paper. In the left corner was emblazoned the letters H A R P E R. Adjacent to the archaic printing was the imprint of a coat of arms, a crest, and a motto. A tattered piece of paper fell away from the parchment. It was a note from their father, with a detailed explanation of what Josiah had in his hand. After reading for a time, the other brother exclaimed.

"Cass, do you know what this is?"

"No, what?"

"This is who we are. Father writes that this is our family arms that shows our heritage and where we came from. This is important. Father must have wanted us to have this some day."

He read: 'ARMS: Argent, a lion rampant with a bordure engrailed sable.

CREST: A boar passant or ducally gorged and crined gules.

Motto: Te deum laudamus.'

"Josiah, what do all those words mean?"

Josiah was smug in that he thought he understood more than his younger brother, and so he began to tell Castleton what he figured out from their father's description of the HARPER COAT OF ARMS.*

"Cass, 'argent' means white or silver, and a lion 'rampant' is a lion that is standing on its hind foot with one foreleg raised about the other and the head in profile. That 'rampant' probably means menacing, wild, or without restraint. 'Engrailed' means it is put on the shield to stay forever, and 'sable' is black. Now, see the boar on top of the shield? Castleton nodded his head. "That means a wild pig, or a fierce, wild animal of some type."

"Good night, are we supposed to be pigs or something?"

"No, Cass. No. It probably means that we are to be fierce, and that we should not have any fear but should be willing to fight until death." He went on, "The word 'ducally' means that the Harpers had something to do with a dukedom or something. You know, Grandmother always did say that we were part of the royalty. Centuries ago, Harpers or Harpurs, as they were called then, used to be officers in the royal courts with their harps playing most of the music. Well, to get on. The word 'gorged' has to mean that we are full of something. I guess it means we should be full of courage. 'Crined' means all of those sharp bends that are on the shield. And the word 'gules' means red, having to do with our shedding blood, I suppose."

"Gosh, that is scary."

"You are right. But I suppose Father meant for us to someday understand all of this."

"What's the motto thing for, Josiah?"

"Those are the words we should live by, Castleton. They are written in Latin and mean 'We praise our God.' Nice, don't you think? We should never forget to offer our praise for his watch-care over us, Castleton."

"Where did all of this, this coat of arms, motto and all come from, Josiah?"

"From our ancestors. Grandmother told me that in 1066 one of our ancestors was knighted by William the Conqueror after the Battle of Hastings.* Then in 1273 the name Henry le Harpur is mentioned in the Cambridge County and Willelemus Harper in the Poll Tax listing in the County of York in 1379.* There is a Rogerus Harper on that same record.* And then there is a Richard Harper.* Well, it's for sure that the name Harpur has been known a long time in England.* Pappa must have wanted us to know all of this."

"You will, Castleton. In years to come, I hope I'll understand more."

With that from the bottom of the steps a lusty shout emitted, "Supper's ready. Come to supper, young Men."

Because they were so hungry, they flew down the steps, and as they approached the table, they suddenly realized they had for-gotten to wash up.

THEIR NEW JOBS

Early the next morning Captain Elsnor came to pick up the boys. All through the night the good man had pondered about where he should take the young men he had more or less taken under his wing. He knew both of them needed gainful employment because in a matter of months he would be taking the DILIGENCE back to England, and he would not be around to look after them. "Mrs.

34

Carlsen will feed them, but they must be schooled in an occupation." And so the trio again set out on the streets of Philadelphia. The boys had no idea where their trusted friend was leading them. They just followed. They were thunderstruck with what they saw milling around the streets of downtown Philadelphia.

Immigrants were everywhere. They remembered the handbills, ballads, and sermons delivered by friendly ministers on the streets of Leicester that glowingly recounted that 'a crock of gold' could be found in America. They presumed everyone in the world had responded affirmatively. Packhorse men, peddlers, those who thought to be planters, or perhaps some kind of swashbuckling adventurer were everywhere. They gazed sadly at families that had servants in tow as they walked the streets. In their minds they pictured their father doing the same. But he was not there. Shaking off their temporary sadness, the boys became enthralled by the sights of blacks, called Negroes, and even red-skinned people they knew to be Indians.

"Are all of these folks workers or indentured, or whatever you call it, Josiah? How can we get a job with so many people here looking for work?" Castleton asked his brother. Both Castleton and Josiah remembered the advertisements in England for workers. "Sign a deed of indenture for a time, and then you will receive a salary and eventually be freed to receive your own land grant." Now that they were in America, such an idea seemed too good to be true. They both itched to own their own land, particularly Josiah. And even Castleton dreamed about it as if he were already a man. But Josiah, who didn't answer Castleton, worried about the sheer quantity of numbers, also. He didn't know how they would ever find a suitable job. He looked hopefully in Captain Elsnor's direction. Churches dotted the corners. People were going in and out of their doors, and while doing so, seemed to create no stir or fright whatsoever. The many churches told the story that the Quakers believed the community must be close knit and have a mutual brotherliness according to Christ's teachings. It could be seen that the church element was striving to establish a godly society rather than a disorderly one as all of the newcomers tried to conquer the wilderness.

The boys made a mental note to attend the Friends' gathering they found closest to Mrs. Carlsen's first thing on Sunday morning.

"Come lads," the captain broke into their thinking. "Let's make haste. There are two gentlemen I wish for you to meet near Dock Street down by the wharves. Noble men, they are. Noble, good men." With that he stepped up his stride and motioned for them to hurry. Castleton almost fell as he stumbled over a high break in the makeshift walkway on the street. He was fascinated by the red man. He could not keep himself from staring at the Indians, particularly since they were the first Indians he had ever seen in his whole life. There were many of them strolling on the streets.

William Penn had an extraordinary ability to get along with the Indians and years before had won their trust. In fact, shortly after his arrival in the new world, he had met a large group of them and gained their respect so much that the tribes were willing to sign what was called "The Great Treaty." As a result Philadelphians, within the city area, had never had to fear the native Americans. They were amazing for the lads to behold.

Their skins were tawny and frequently daubed with bear's oil of a color like burnt cork. Their hair was long and seemed to be greased with some kind of oil. For the most part they were tall, sedate, and walked with a kind of majesty. Castleton had read that they had the best eyes of any humans because they burned pitch pine in their wigwams. They certainly did look strong. Their legs looked firm and muscular as if they could run, travel, and hunt for hours without getting tired. Staring, he thought the Indians he saw had kind, almost sweet faces. It was hard to believe that the same red man walking the streets in Philadelphia was reputed to have scalped, killed, or even roasted his enemy. Castleton shuddered. Never, did he want to fight an Indian.

"Come on lad," Captain Elsnor pulled on his shirt. "We haven't got all day for you to stand and daydream about them Indians. We've got to be going."

"Sorry, sir. Sorry." And the young lad hastened after his benefactor.

They had walked a while and finally in the midst of the floods of people the captain motioned them into a shop that read on the front glass, "Hans Scmidt, Printer."

"This is one of my German friends," Captain Elsnor said as he directed the two young men into the door.

"Hans, Hans Scmidt, this is Hamilton Elsnor here. Elsnor."

Whereupon the printer in the rear of the shop dropped the tools of his trade and hastened forward. "Captain, Captain, my friend." He came from around the counter and gave his friend a mighty embrace. "I had heard that the DILIGENCE had docked. What a good fortune that I get to see you. Truly this is a blessing from God." And he continued, "I prayed for your safe journey, Captain. I prayed to our eternal God. My vision was that you were in desperate straits, and that the ship that brought me to this paradise almost foundered. Tell me, Captain, is that true? Is that what almost happened?"

"Aye, Hans. Aye. It was a desperate journey. But through God's goodness we have arrived. And," as he motioned toward Josiah and Castleton, "these are my friends, the Harper brothers, Josiah and Castleton. Josiah is an able-bodied man, and I think would do well in the printing business. He is all of sixteen going on seventeen. He is very well educated, Hans, and an articulate, young man." He laughed. "At least I think he is." I had hoped that you could find a position for him. Of course, he would be willing to sign an indenture with you." He smiled expectantly at the printer.

"Nonsense, nonsense. We will discuss that later. Of course, of course I will make a position for the young man. I can already see in his eyes that someday he will be a great editor, a great publisher." He laughed heartily and clapped the young man on the shoulder.

Elsnor felt a great relief. Thanking his German friend, he left the shop. Hans insisted that Josiah start working right away, and so the young man jumped into his chores with great alacrity. He was thrilled beyond words that he had secured a position.

Castleton looked up at his captain friend with wondering eyes as if to say, "What about me, Captain. Where can I work?"

But the captain was ahead of him and two doors down from the print shop entered a bake shop, on which was written, James Stephens, Baker.* He was also an old immigrant that the DILIGENCE had brought to America. And he, too, was thrilled to see the old captain. Before the afternoon was over Castleton had been hired by the baker for an indenture of four years.* After four years the young lad would be fifteen; or as he would say, "going on 16." At such time Castleton would be eligible for a land grant. Then his future in the new world would begin!

That night Captain Elsnor slept soundly. He had at last succeeded in providing for the young boys that he had assumed personal responsibility for so many weeks before.

Six weeks later, the DILIGENCE, with its cracks and joints resealed, the hold scoured, hoisted its sails and left the harbor of Philadelphia to begin its journey back to the faraway shores of England. With regret he left the Harper brothers behind. But with prayers in his heart he felt that God would grant them a special blessing and grant them a long, prosperous and happy life in the new land.

The Harper brothers had gathered before the break of dawn to watch the departure of THE DILIGENCE. As the ship sailed away, they waved, and kept waving until the figure of their newly adopted father, Captain Hamilton Elsnor, vanished from their sight. They were alone. And there was no one to depend upon but each other and their Almighty God.

With a sigh they turned from the docks and made their way to the printing shop and bakery. Resolved to be real men, and not to show overt emotion, they went about their daily work, and they were unwilling to speak of the fear and doubt that lay low in the pit of their stomachs.

THE BIRTH OF HARPERS' WEEKLY

Two years after the departure of the DILIGENCE in 1726 Josiah met Castleton after a long day of labor. They trudged wearily through the darkening streets toward the Carlsen's.

"You know," said Josiah, "I can imagine that the captain would be pleased to know that we have been doing as well as we have, Cass. Thank our good God we have been able finally to give Mrs. Carlsen some money for our lodging. I am certainly glad. It was only fair even though she never did want to take our money."

"Josiah," said the young Castleton, now much taller than two years previously and quite full of stature. "I plan to continue to pay her as long as my indenture is going on, after that I might want to leave Philadelphia and go on out to meet Uncle John, you know … the place Father wanted us to go in the first place. I am sure Uncle John will be able to direct our path as to what we should do in the future."

"Castleton," said Josiah as he stopped his brother and looked full into his eyes. "I have been wanting to tell you this for some time; I haven't really known how. Mr. Scmidt, you know, never did have me sign a note of indenture." All of a sudden the words started to spill rapidly from his mouth. "Anyhow, this man came in the print shop from New York City the other day, and we got to talking about printing and editing opportunities up in New York. Well, to make a long story short, he wants me to come to New York and start writing for his newspaper, THE WEEKLY JOURNAL. His name is Peter Zenger, and he wants to start this newspaper in the next few years. He thinks I can help him." He finished rather lamely. "It would mean leaving you, Cass. What do you think?"

Castleton was momentarily taken aback, and then with a flash in his eye and a tilt of his head as if to indicate his manliness he answered. "Josiah, I think you ought to go. Don't worry about me. I will be fine, and I will stay with Mrs. Carlsen until my indenture is over. Then I think I will go down to the southeast to Oxford and meet up with Uncle John. I will be fine, really. I want you to go." He quickly walked ahead of his brother. He did not want him to see the tears that were filling in his eyes. Nor did he want to admit the lack of courage that actually he felt a part of his soul. Could he ever make it without Josiah? Would he ever make it? Castleton thought to himself that there was no question. He had to go on alone. And Josiah had to make his way to his future.

By the time they reached the Carlsen's, the shock of his brother's announcement had lessened somewhat, and Castleton was ready to meet the new challenge of 'living alone' with resolve and courage.

"Josiah, when will you be going? Soon?"

"Mr. Zenger wants me to be ready to go in a fortnight. What do you think? Should I go?"

"Absolutely. You probably won't get this chance again. Absolutely!"

The matter was settled. On the evening of the next day the two boys met for the last time in their upstairs' room. The looked at each other, and gave each other a last embrace.

Castleton put his gold coin in Josiah's hands. "Josiah, please take my gold coin. You might be needing it in New York."

"No, Cass. One is for you. You must have it. When you get a new settlement, you will probably need it to buy something very important. I won't take it."

At that point Josiah handed Castleton three things, the parchment with the coat of arms, their Father's old Bible, and a small Testament that belonged to their mother. When Castleton saw the small Testament, he was surprised.

"That's Mother's. Where did you find it?"

"I didn't, Cass. The captain found it when he was cleaning up the hold of the ship, and he gave it to me some time back. I forgot to tell you."

"Josiah, I can't take all of these things with me. I can't. They're yours."

"No, my dear brother. You will be the one to go into the wilderness. You will need all three of these things for your sustenance, for your hope, and for your promise. Father and Mother would want you to have them."

The matter was settled. The next morning the two of them walked to Elizabeth Town Point where Josiah's ship would depart for Murray's Wharf at the foot of Wall Street in New York.

The two young men clung to each other desperately for a moment. Seeing his new benefactor, John Peter Zenger, on board the ship, Josiah hastened aboard.

40

It was the last time that Castleton Harper, now Castleton Harper, Sr., would see his brother Josiah. It was reported to Castleton years later that indeed John Peter Zenger had established a newspaper in New York in 1733 called THE WEEKLY JOURNAL, and that Josiah had been one of his main workers in the project.

Some years later, Josiah Harper began his own weekly publication.* It was called HARPER'S WEEKLY, a Journal of Civilization.* It was established in New York City on Franklin's Square.*

THE LAST OF PHILADELPHIA

The four years of indenture of Castleton Harper to James Stephens finally came to an end. For two years after the departure of Josiah to New York, Castleton worked diligently and saved much of his money, which he hoarded and stored in his father's backpack.

"Wherever I go, old pack, you will go too." He gave the pack a hard swat as he stashed another of his weekly earnings deep within its recesses. He was grateful he lived at Mrs. Carlsen's away from rapacious eyes that might seek to steal his earthly treasure. As for Mrs. Carlsen, he had become terribly fond of the good, portly woman. Actually, Mrs. Carlsen considered Castleton her adopted son, although she was too proud to show him any signs of outward affection. While he did relate to Mrs. Carlsen, other than her, Castleton led a solitary life. Mr. Stephens had been a good employer, and he would be forever indebted to him. But as his fifteenth birthday drew near, the young Harper lad more than once turned to the southwest where he felt new challenges and a new life beckoning.

His favorite place for resting and musing in Philadelphia was on the banks of the Schuylkill where he would sit and watch small boats float up and down the river for hours. On the Schuylkill near a street called Front Street was a ramshackle toll bridge owned by the Brothers G. and R. Gray. He was fascinated by the traffic and the people that mounted the old bridge bound for the other side of the river and adventure. Little did he know that in 1789, a regal gentleman known as George Washington would cross the same bridge on a gorgeous, white horse. Banners on the bridge would read, 'Don't Tread On Me,' and small girls would perch on an arch to be constructed at the foot of the bridge where they would sit dropping laurels and flowers on the new leader of the free world. The dusty road that approached the bridge would be lined with people, and George Washington, in his brilliant blue coat, would sit astride his horse and wave to the throng. Little did Castleton know that his favorite resting place while in Philadelphia would know the presence of this famed soldier of the future. In fact, until the new government was established in Washington, D. C., Philadelphia would be the headquarters of the new fledgling nation. But Castleton was unaware of the place's historical signif-icance. Such was far in the future. He had enjoyed the arrival of a man called Benjamin Franklin into Philadelphia. It was rumored that he had traveled all the way from Boston, and that he was going to do a lot of planning for all of the colonies, which would help them some day be free from mother England.

With all of his time spent working, and his free time sleep-ing, doing a bit of reading, and investigating various places in Philadelphia, Castleton had little or no time to dwell on such political matters. He had more important things on his mind.

"Well, Cass, my friend, old man," he talked to himself. "Soon you will be able to leave Mr. Stephens. It's time you looked to getting some gear together, and a horse for the trail." Oxford, Pennsylvania was the destination he had in mind. He had thought of writing his Uncle John so he would expect him, but he decid-ed against it. He decided he would probably arrive before his letter. He began to ask around about the route to Oxford. Perhaps he was following himself, he wondered frequently, but he soon decided that he was well-enough versed in the direction he should go, and that he had nothing to fear about getting lost.

Counting his meager savings, he found that as soon as his contract with the baker ended, he would have sufficient funds to buy his horse of adventure. He settled on a gentle, big bay horse. He liked it. And the horse seemed to respond to his touch. When he considered his limited experience in horsemanship, Castleton knew he needed the most reliable, not the fastest, but the calmest horse he could buy.

Often he thought about his ancestors. Would he have the courage to face the unknown as they did in the Battle of Hastings? He doubted it. Or what was it that Josiah had told him before he left? One of their ancestors had fought in the Crusades in Israel in the 1300's. Amazing, he thought to himself many times, the amount of courage and the lack of fear they must have had.

"I need to be more like a wild pig, I suppose. Fierce, and unafraid. Well, I suppose I can try. One thing I really need to do more of though is shout to Heaven, 'I praise you, oh God!'" more than once came from his lips and flowed through his thoughts.

The particular night before leaving as he went to bed, he gathered up his Father's Bible, and read underlined passages in it about safe deliverance from evil, and then reread and traced the words of the Harpers' crest ... 'to be unafraid.' He wondered if he would succeed.

WESTWARD

On a warm, sunny morning in early fall on September 1, 1726, Castleton Harper formerly a Junior, but now a Senior, mounted his newly purchased horse, said his last farewells to the few people in Philadelphia that he had allowed himself to meet, and began his journey to the west, southwest, in search of a settlement called Oxford, Pennsylvania, purported to be founded by his father's brother, John, in the late 1680's.*

Castleton was happy to be leaving Philadelphia, although he would miss Mr. Stephens, and particularly his motherly friend, Lydia Carlsen. She was almost beside herself with grief. Trying to supplant her sorrow, she cooked and backed for him for days. Laden with supplies and her foodstuffs packed into his bag, he departed.

"Sure, and when Captain Elsnor returns and you are gone, Lad, he will be saddened to know that you have left for parts unknown. But then, young Man, you must be about the future, that I know, even though I will miss you sorely, indeed. May God go with you wherever you shall be, and my prayers will be with you Lad, always, always." Weeping in her apron, Mrs. Carlsen patted his arm, and gave an affectionate pat to the rump of Castleton's bay horse. She went tramping back into the only home that Castleton ever had known in the new world.

As he guided his horse through the streets, he couldn't help but think about the changes that even he had seen in his brief residency in the City of Brotherly Love. The dock near the bakery was more of a beehive than ever. Manufactured goods from Europe were arriving constantly, and booming businesses of rum distilling, rope walks, sail lofts, and all kinds of things relating to the sea had sprung up. Castleton had met scores of craftsmen, retailers, innkeepers and small jobbers that were pouring into the burgeoning Philadelphia. He often wondered if those folks missed England or their homeland. Surely the women did, and perhaps the children, for with the men came families, of women, children and scores of servants. Some of them looked so young, Castleton often wondered if they had been 'trapanned.' Mrs. Carlsen told him those were children that had been kidnapped from their families in the old country. Many of the young ones looked very frightened and lonely. Perhaps they had been spirited aboard ships bound for the new world. Castleton hoped not. He looked at them with concern and sorrow in his heart. On the dock previously Castleton had met rebels and even convicts that roamed the streets in large numbers. Of course, the many ships brought many sailors from everywhere. The sails, together with all of the unemployed and unskilled workers that ran the streets, disturbed Mr. Stephens mightily. Many times the unwitting baker had been bilked and robbed by the like. As he led his horse away from Philadelphia, Castleton decided it was not a pretty time in the life of Philadelphia. It was a good time to leave. He was glad he was on horseback, because many of the dirt roads (only the downtown streets had been paved), were muddy and rutted from recent heavy rains. Big potholes were everywhere.

The night before his departure he had painstakingly sewn his gold coin in the lining of his coat. The gold coin was his pass to economic prosperity in the future. Of that he was convinced. With the riffraff running rampant he was most cautious as he tried to protect his few meager earnings from pilfering. As he mounted his new purchase, the bay horse, he felt secure in his decision to move out and onward. He had promised Josiah that he was going to do so, and too, he felt as though he was living out the dream of his father to be reunited once again with Uncle John in Oxford.

Before his departure Castleton considered delaying his trip until springtime when the weather would be more mild. But the fall days had been warm and lazy, even though there was the promise of a fall's frost in the air. When he received his papers from the baker, he had to leave. To wait for springtime would have been impossible. And so, off he went, in spite of the dangers of the trail and the vagaries of an approaching winter.

He had talked to others and had been told that en route to the settlement of Oxford, about 60 miles southwest of Philadelphia, there would be several settlements that he would find, Kennett's Square and Chadd's Ford. If he found these places, he could be assured that he was on the right trail. However, he had been warned that if he got as far west as Octoraro Creek he would have overshot his destination. He knew he would cross many creeks. But he wondered how he would know the names of any of them.

He was determined to make Oxford in three, maybe four days' time. He thought he could if he did not wander from the trail, get lost, or have any other mishaps. He was trusting that such would be the case. Alone, outfitted with supplies for three days, a warm, great coat that Mrs. Carlsen had donated, and a fledgling knowledge of the direction in which he was headed, the young pioneer started off.

He admitted later to his uncle, that crossing the Schuylkill on the rickety bridge owned by the Gray brothers at the beginning of the trip was so frightening to him and his horse that he almost turned around and went back. But he managed to cross the bridge safely, as he said "by the grace of God."

Autumn in Pennsylvania was idyllic on a sunny day. After riding through a large portion of the Atlantic coast plain through which more than ninety percent of Pennsylvania's land area drained, primarily the Delaware and Susquehanna Rivers, Castleton made his way through bogs and shallow estuaries for most of his first day. It was fortunate, he thought, that the weather had been clear and nice, and not foggy as was often the case along the shoreline. He enjoyed the warmish, cool breeze that came in from the bay, and marveled at the brilliant colors of wild cranberry growing in the bogs, at the calls of the seabirds and the land birds, and the occasional mink, muskrat, or beaver jumping in and out of their wooden lairs built in the sea-tide pools. Once or twice he caught sight of Indians with their lines cast into the water as they fished for their food. He didn't stop to converse with any of them but hailed them with a wave. They seemed friendly enough and answered his gesture with a friendly tilt of their heads or a bend of their arms. At first, as night approached, he wondered where he would be able to camp for the evening. The land was marshy and wet. But as nighttime came on, he was relieved that the terrain had changed, and that he was riding out of the wet, coast land area and was soon climbing into the foothills of Pennsylvania. As nightfall came, he found himself in the beginning of the gently rolling hills of a piedmont area replete with ample places to bed down for the night. He was thankful to God once again that he had been delivered, and after a quick ration around a fire, he bedded down for the night. He pulled his horse close to the campfire. He wanted him tethered where he could hear anything that might happen, or anyone that might come close. To say he was unafraid would be a lie. He was frightened to death.

The sounds of the night struck the neophyte camper with fear. More than once he heard rustling. White-tailed deer came into the light of the fire, noted the intruder in their domain, and then darted into the gathering darkness. He heard more distinct rustling in the brush beyond his fire, roused to refurbish it, and once again fell into a troubled sleep. The next morning he felt a cold chill when he saw the footprints of a huge bear around the campsite.

Thankful to the Almighty that he had survived the first night, he mounted his horse again early the morning of the second day. From his makeshift map he decided that he would soon be approaching Kennett Square. Getting his bearings from the rising sun, he again thanked God for his deliverance. Again, he was overwhelmed with the beauty of the wilderness. As his horse made a climb on a steady incline that showed he was in the foothills of the Pocono Mountains, Castleton knew why the entire beautiful state had been nicknamed "Penn's Woods." The lowlands had melted into a continuous forest. He marveled at the myriad of autumn colors on the plethora of hardwood trees that speckled the low-lying hills. He didn't know the names of most of them, but after a while he could identify a few.

"Thank God that Father taught me all about God's creation, especially about some of His magnificent trees!" He was familiar with the dogwood. The dogwood on the hillside were a crimson red, while hemlock and gigantic bushes of what he learned later to be mountain laurel, and azaleas hugged the sides of the rocky crevices over which his horse skillfully traversed. In early afternoon he spotted the fires of a settlement. His horse seemed to gather speed as the two of them trotted down to a comfortable enclosure set in the middle of a rocky plateau. As he rode through some makeshift gates, he saw lettered on some roughhewn boards, Kennett's Square. It had a population of eighteen. Three families made up the entirety of the village. It was situated on a swift running creek that provided the area with ample drinking water. The fields and the meadows beyond were lush with wild flowers, and several cultivated areas of crops, no doubt to be harvested for the subsistence of the villagers. They were most cordial to the wandering lad.

"Come thee, young lad, into our humble abode. Dwell with us, and we will be most pleased to offer thee food and lodging." The man. who seemed to be the titular head of the small colony, was most insistent.

"No Sir. I cannot stay. But I will be happy to join you in a small repast. That would be most generous and kind of you." Castleton smiled at the gracious people.

Whereupon the wife and young daughter of the older man scurried into one of the cabins, and soon Castleton could see the smoke emitting from its roof and the scents of cooking wafting through the air.

"Care for a smoke?" The man handed Castleton a carved-out pipe.

"No thank you, Sir." I have not as yet taken of tobacco."

"Ah, yes. Thou art a wise, young man. Wise. My name is Kennett, Clyde Kennett, at your service, young sir. And what might be thine name?"

Castleton proceeded to give him all the information about himself and his intended destination and what his past had been and his plans for the future.

Finally, Castleton finished with, "and that is why, Mr. Kennett, I cannot abide here with you for the evening. I must make haste for my destination." With that a call from the cabin interrupted the two men as they made their way into the table.

"Bless our young guest, our great and good Father, and bless him on his way, I pray." The blessing was said, and a delicious meal of baked, wild turkey, and cranberry pudding was enjoyed.

Clyde Kennett continued, "Yes, Castleton, my friend, you should be making Chadd's Ford by tomorrow at sunset, and then perchance you will make your destination on the evening of the next day. Perhaps you are not allowing yourself enough time, but with God's grace, you will arrive sufficiently."

"I realize, Mr. Kennett, that my goal for a three-day journey was a bit ambitious. But perchance my aspirations will prevail, and my schedule will be realized."

Not long thereafter Castleton told his newly-found friends farewell; after a tearful goodbye, the lonely settlers of Kennett Square bid their only guest for many days, weeks, and months, goodbye.

That night in the foothills of the Poconos the traveling pilgrim camped with a bit more ease and courage. As night fell, it seemed to him that the wind had risen, and that the warmer day was being replaced by a cold, damp chill.

The next day the sun was replaced by a grey sky and threatening clouds. The wind was cutting and chilling. Castleton prayed that he would reach his destination before he froze to death. The elevation of his journey had changed from about 100 feet to almost 1000 and with that the temperature had dropped significantly. He pulled his greatcoat tighter around his body as he thanked God for its warmth, and Mrs. Carlsen. His trusty horse went between hilltops and the bottoms of valleys. Each time he road down to a valley he prayed that soon he would see Chadd's Ford, which was a small settlement on the banks of a tumbling creek, or so Clyde Kennett had told him. On the top of one ridge he heard a roaring stream, rode a bit further, and almost stumbled down into a huge drop-off cliff. From the side of the hill a gigantic waterfall was falling. It careened down the hill more than 100 feet until it reached the valley below.

"Surely somewhere on this creek, I will find Chadd's Ford."

The horse picked its way down the hillside. All Castleton could hear was the roaring of the waterfall and the tumbling of the creek on the rocks below. He had been traveling five or ten miles along the shore of the creek, when he heard laughing. Suddenly, two children ran from the trees, as they laughingly jumped along the rocky shoreline of the brook. They were playing. When they saw the horseman, they stopped short. Surprised, shouting to one another, they ran ahead to a clearing about a mile up the branch. It was Chadd's Ford.

At this point the water was tumbling with pillows of white foam over innumerable rocks. Castleton could see that a woven footbridge had been built over the water for anyone attempting to ford the creek. He assumed it was Chadd's Ford. It was.

As in Kinnett's Square, he was greeted with open arms and treated like royalty. The settlers of the wilderness, Castleton found, hungered for new faces and any word about the world they had left behind. They gathered around Castleton as he recounted the story of his journey, about his trip over the ocean, and particularly about life in Philadelphia. The ladies' eyes seem to sparkle when he described the busy, frenetic businesses and the men and women in Philadelphia. The women were entranced with tales of silk frocks, feathered hats, and all of those niceties that the stalwart women of the frontier had left behind months and years before. Chadd's Ford was a relaxing respite for Castleton. Because of the cold weather and the threat of snow, he agreed to spend the night in the settlement. As he nestled in one of their warm beds, he wondered to himself, "Might I have been better off to have stayed in Philadelphia and become a prosperous business man?" As the winds blew around the little settlement, soon the tired bedraggled traveler, content with the knowledge that he was doing the right thing, and that the best was yet to be in his life ahead, drifted off. He had been assured that he had not yet found Octoraro Creek, and that it was miles distant from Chadd's Ford.

Early the next morning with the blessings and prayers of the small Quaker encampment on the banks of the creek, the young traveler and his horse started off again on the trail. His spirits lifted, as the air seemed to clear and warm up somewhat. He felt secure in the knowledge that he was going in the right direction, and before long he would be reunited with his Uncle John and his family whom he had not seen for many years. He thanked God moment by moment for his safe journey and his deliverance on the trail.

The fog had not completely cleared. The terrible happened. Castleton and his horse had just rounded the trail that was bordered on one side by a giant boulder when something leaped on him from above and drove a searing pain through his back as he was thrown from his horse. His assailant was a smelly, filthy man. Soon, two more joined the attacker, as they pounced upon the hapless victim. Castleton was clubbed senseless. He was beaten mercilessly. His spooked horse galloped away taking with it all of his supplies for the trail. Castleton tried to ward off the blows. Soon he was no longer aware of his surroundings. Blackness fell upon him. The whiskey-ridden robbers pillaged the journeyman's pockets, and finally satisfied that they had succeeded in ravaging their victim as much as possible, stumbled off into the shadows of the fog. All that could be heard were the sounds of their horses trotting away, and the echo of their insane laughter.

Castleton lay on the forest floor in a crumpled ball, unconscious and almost dead.

DELIVERANCE

The day proceeded. He lay inert on the trail of the pine forest. All that could be heard were the sounds of the birds calling in the trees, and the occasional rustle of an animal in the brush. The cool wind of the morning had freshened a bit. An icy chill began to settle in the hills. The silence was broken by the shuffle of padded feet on the needles nestled in the soil. Two men approached carrying a heavy load up the precipitous hill. They were Indians. Between them they bore the carcass of a freshly killed deer. Warily they approached the body of the man lying in the path. In their Indian language they conversed.

"Nokomo, what is that we see? White man, Nokomo. White man!" As he spoke, he gently nudged the lifeless form and looked up at his traveling companion.

"Ah, Manamoo, man hurt. Hurt bad. Alive, Manamoo, alive?" he questioned the other.

"Much hurt, but the fire is still there. Quick, we must get some sticks and lift him aboard and carry him to the village. Suekawa can help. She can make him well. Hurry!"

Wrapping the white man in several skins to warm the frigid body, the two Indians hurriedly constructed a makeshift litter that they attached to their waists with stout leather thongs. On their shoulders they continued to carry the deer they had slaughtered for meat. Slowly pulling the litter behind them, the braves made their way over the hills. When they came to creeks, they would first carry the litter over the water, and then come back for their kill. They were tempted to leave the meat behind. But with the coming winter quickly setting in, they knew their tribe was in desperate need for rations, and they could not afford to allow any game they had killed to be left behind.

Before the sun had set, they reached a village that set on the banks of a roaring creek. The area was bustling with activity. Tall, male Indians convocated in groups, while both tiny and large children ran around the skirts of their working mothers. As the tribe viewed the kill of the two braves, they were cheered. But then, the band noticed the litter. As the two braces with the litter in tow hurried to one of the long houses, a hush fell over the village. With fear they viewed the lifeless body of a white man.

In stern tones the Indian called Manamoo spoke. "Away. Make room. Man much hurt. Much hurt. Suekawa make well. We take."

The curious crowd parted as the two Indian braves entered a long, rectangular, straw hut.

"Quick, Nokomo, Suekawa is here." They entered the dark interior of a long, straw house. In one area there was a divided section that evidently housed Suekawa and her family. "Suekawa, man hurt. Bad hurt. You make well. You can do." Nokomo and Manamoo gently lifted the wounded man off of the litter and laid him on a pallet at the old, Indian squaw's feet.

Suekawa was a short-statured, Indian woman, whose long plaited hair was streaked with grey. Her leathered, line face was ageless. Only with the darting of her dark, brown eyes would the average stranger realize that this woman, although old, had exceptional brightness, wisdom, and as the braves believed, the magic power of healing.

Still not speaking, the Indian squaw looked at the lifeless form of a young, white man. He did not move. She thought he might be dead. But then again, as she touched him, she knew that in him was still a spark of life. Methodically she set about to rekindle the flame. Her lips parted and with her brown, stained teeth, two of which were missing in the front, she spoke. "Away, away. Suekawa, she fix." She motioned the two braves out of her quarters, and with eyes of respect, the two braves backed gingerly away from her.

That night the north wind began to blow. The natives huddled in their long houses, each family close together by the fire that burned brightly in the center of each of the long house sections. Winter was coming. The temperature plummeted.

The days to follow were days of ice and cold, wind and sleet. The Indians all donned robes made from animal skins, mittens, and fur caps. Ice topped the rocks in the creek nearby. The roar of the water was unceasing.

The days dragged on into weeks, and the weeks into months. At times the Indian braves would leave the camp. Infrequently one would return with a snowshoe rabbit or a bird that they might happen upon. Suekawa ventured from her quarters seldom. Her time was taken by her vigil over the white man. The power within her knew that he was improving, even though he had not yet spoken. But his eyes had opened. He stared at her without comprehension. She knew then that she had found the spark within him, and that soon it would revive.

At first when the white man became more cognizant of his surroundings, he reacted with fear. But soon he realized he was in the tender arms of a deliverer. He was at peace. Gradually he began to regain his strength. He sat up for the first time in many, many days. As he sat up, he was so weak that he almost fell over again on the floor, but the old Indian woman propped him up in her arms.

Castleton Harper was going to live. After a long time he could acknowledge the fact that he was amid a large group of Indians, Indians that had saved his life. Unable to understand their language, he understood their kindness. He could only catch names, like Nokomo, Manamoo, and his benefactor, Suekawa.

After a while Castleton regained his strength. Finally, he was able to remember the details of the attack on the path in the forest. Immediately he wanted to gather up his things, tell his deliverers goodbye, and be on his way to his Uncle John. But it was not that simple. As he looked out of the long hut, he knew the trails and the forest were impassable. Winter was in full sway. He would have to bide his time. It was just as well. Despite his apparent recovery, Castleton had a terrible weakness whenever he tried to walk. He was grounded. He had to get well before he could navigate on his own. Of this he was sure. He could not tell his Indian friends about his plans, for he could not communicate with them. Often at night when he sat among them around the fire, he gazed into the embers and considered his lot. He was penniless. The robbers had stolen all of his savings from his money belt, and his black, greatcoat had disappeared. He needed the warmth of his great coat, but more than that his heart broke to think that the gold coin he had sewn in the lining was gone forever. Too, the coat of arms that he had so carefully folded in his pack, was no more.

He had no horse. Nothing. The severe winter did nothing to dispel his discouragement. However, as soon as the weather broke, he felt better. Castleton was up and about in the village. He noted that the tribe lived in long houses rather than teepees as he had thought all Indians did. They hunted caribou, moose, deer and elk for food, but they also subsisted on wild plants, berries and nuts. As he watched the Indian men with their long skin shirts and high, breech clothes of leggings and moccasins, Castleton was awed by their strength and their apparent resiliency. He decided that the Indian would be able to deal with anything and everything.

At long last Castleton knew that he was strong enough to travel. But he was confused about where to go, and certainly how he would get to his destination. He had no map. He had no horse. Time and again when he tried to talk with with his young Indian friends, Nokomo and Manamoo, he would repeat the word, 'Oxford.' Then he would gesture westward, as if he was pleading with the red men to show him the way. Miraculously in time the two braves seemed to understand, and one day laughingly indicated that they certainly knew the way to a place called 'Oxford.' They seemed to understand that the white friend whose life they had saved was ready to ride away, to leave their village.

One brilliant morning Castleton was awaken by the neighing of a horse. Outside of the hut in which he was sleeping was tethered a beautiful bay horse. It was his very own. On top of it lay a giant, black coat. It was his very own. Piled on top of the horse were blankets and supplies for the trail. If it would have been manly, Castleton Harper would have cried. But Castleton had to keep his emotional turmoil hidden. In a matter of minutes most of the tribe appeared, and with a customary grace befitting their people, gave the young pioneer a sendoff he would never forget all of his living days. Two stallions with his Indian friends astride waited to lead him and the big bay down the trail toward Oxford. When the red men were certain their friend would not get lost, they quickly disappeared into the woods. Nokomo and Manamoo were seen no more.

OXFORD

Not too many days after leaving his Indian friends Castleton Harper trotted into Oxford, Pennsylvania. His heart was beating so wildly he almost fainted as he rushed to meet the first white man he had seen since leaving Kinnett's Square. He wanted to kiss the soil because he knew that he had arrived home, the first time he could call a place home since he had left his loft in England. The thought of finally meeting his Uncle John was almost more than he could bear.

The first settler he met was almost as dumbfounded as Castleton was to see a perfect stranger appear from the woods, a white man at that! Castleton was the first to speak. "Harper here. Castleton Harper. I am John Harper's nephew. I would like to see my Uncle John. I come from Philadelphia."

The astounded settler dropped the hoe that he had been carrying and with a broad smile directed the young lad to one of several square, log buildings. The log house was in the center of a large clearing. Wild, yellow daisies with brilliant black centers glowed in the sunlight around the building. "Brother John, Brother John!" The surprised settler shouted into the cabins as he motioned Castleton to follow him. "You have a visitor, a visitor from Philadelphia! He says he is your nephew!"

Entering the cool recesses of a darkened cabin, Castleton's eyes at first could not adjust to what he saw. But then he saw a tall, slender, grey-bearded man rise from a chair and slowly make his way toward the young traveler. Crippled with rheumatism, the older gentleman hobbled toward him with his arms outstretched.

"Son? Son?" he questioned, seemingly confused and taken aback.

"Castleton, Sir. Castleton Harper. My father's name was Castleton also. I am his son!"

Whereupon the older man threw himself around the younger man. "Castleton? Castleton's son? This I cannot believe." Whereupon he wept with racking sobs.

"Uncle John. Uncle John," the younger man patted him in an effort to comfort him. Whereupon the old man broke out in a radiant smile and hastened Castleton to a waiting chair. Drying his eyes, he finally found his voice. "Oh, son, if thou couldst know the days thy humble servant has spent upon his knees all the while praying that the Almighty would deliver thy humble servant's brother and his family to thy humble servant's door. The hours, the days!" he raved. "But thy father? Thy father? Thy humble servant must see him." He hobbled toward the door.

"Uncle John, wait. Wait, Uncle John!" Castleton took him by the arm and led him back to his chair. "I will tell you what has happened. There is only myself. I am the only one. Only by God's eternal grace did I even manage to arrive here." Questions were about to pour out of the old man's mouth. "Wait, Uncle John. Rest. I will tell you all." With smiles but mostly tears pouring down his cheeks, Castleton Harper proceeded to tell his father's brother of the happy times, but also the times of great sorrow that had transpired.

After hours of his monologue with interspersed questions by his elderly uncle, Castleton stopped. He was bone-weary. Sensing it, his uncle called to someone to feed the young man and show him to a bunk. As he left the cabin, Castleton gave his long-lost uncle an embrace and retired to his newly-found abode. He was asleep in an instant.

In the days ahead Castleton's uncle told him about the beginnings of the tiny village of Oxford. "At first, my son, there were four families that came with thy humble servant. Now there are ten, thirty-nine and twenty-one children." His gaze did not waver from Castleton's face. "Always thy father was aware of thy humble servant's desire to leave England for the new world. He never knew when. After thy humble servant moved from Derby to Oxford, all touch was lost with thy father. There were letters, but little else. Thy father did not know why or when the journey to the new land was begun. The decision was made overnight. Thy humble servant's good, Christian friend, Sir William Penn, found out they thy humble servant was to be hung by order of the Church of England and the Parliament." He looked up at Castleton as he watched the revelation cause his nephew's eyebrows to raise. "It was because of my work with the Friends, the new religious group, thou knowest? It was a very terrible time. For thy humble servant God intervened. Even though thy humble servant was a wanted man by the Church of England, God would not allow evil to prevail. When Brother Penn discovered the royals' plan for thy humble servant's execution, he warned thy humble servant and simultaneously gave thy servant's family a deed to this tract of land in the new world. 'Leave Oxford at once'! was his command." With great effort and an obvious sadness he continued. "There was no time to consider or debate. Thy humble servant and family had to go, then, right away. Many times thy humble servant didst wish to inform thy father of what was about to befall this hapless pilgrim, but circumstances did not allow. Immediacy of action was paramount. The Almighty prevailed. Thy humble servant had to leave Oxford before daybreak." Tearfully his recollection continued. "On the next morning many of thy humble servant's friends were arrested, beaten and eventually hung! It was too terrible! Canst thou believe? Because of a servant's work in the church, arrest and hanging! Thanks to Almighty God's providence and the warning of thy humble servant's friend, escape was made possible that very night. Thy humble servant, together with a good wife and children, left Oxford. The night was at its darkest." He breathed a heavy sigh. "God brought deliverance to this family and bade thy humble servant come here, to Penn's Woods." The old man gestured widely as he resumed his story. "Thusly this, thy humble servant's village, was begun. With God's grace all that is seen has been cleared from the virgin forest." He seemed to catch a second breath. "Never did thy humble servant wish for charity from Brother Penn, Castleton, but rather felt obligated to pay for the man's generosity. Over the objections of thy worthy servant, Brother Penn has accepted only 100 francs for all of the acreage, and a rental of one cent an acre for two hundred acres. 'Tis a pittance then and now. Thy humble servant's protestations have been to no avail. However, now Oxford is a tidewater plantation. The Muscovy Company in England owns the property, Castleton. It is good. Thanks to the company's encouragement, more families are migrating here. It is also providing us with money for development." He nodded. "Oh yes, there is a price to pay for all of this. The colony's abundance is shipped to England for the company's profit. It is a worthy endeavor, methinks, and a good way to go. Thy humble servant only prays that his friend, Brother Penn, will also benefit from the company's proceeds. Methinks he is a member of the company. Fur trading with Indian friends certainly has been a boon to the company." He finished speaking with a grunt of satisfaction. "God has blessed Oxford richly." Castleton sensed that he had been dismissed. Rather amazed that he had been taken into the old man's confidence as he divulged not only information about his past, but also information about the business prosperity of the colony, Castleton hurriedly stepped out into the sunshine. He looked up into the bright sunshine and blue sky, and thanked God that he was once again within the embrace of family. Too long, he thought to himself, he had been a single wayfarer. He loved people. Especially, he realized how very much he loved his newly-found uncle.

As the young man got up to leave, he noticed that the older gentleman was soon nodding in his chair. John Harper dozed off for the afternoon.

Later Castleton learned that John Harper had come over to the new world with the first of William Penn's settlers with gifts of five thousand acres in an area in the southeastern part of the large expanse of land that would be known as Penn's Woods plus a city lot in Philadelphia which Castleton never knew existed.

Frequently his uncle and his family would visit Philadelphia and stay for a period of time. Castleton wished he'd known that his uncle had been so near while in Philadelphia.

The grant from William Penn had saved the life of John Harper and his family. It had been a godsend. John Harper thanked God not only for being saved from certain death, but for the bountiful land he had received from his friend. The acreage seemed to reach forever. The land was beautiful, rich, fertile, and highly productive.

When Castleton Harper rode in on his horse that afternoon in 1728, John Harper, graying and up in years, was flabbergasted. He could not believe that even one of his dear family from England had arrived and survived the journey from abroad.

CASTLETON'S LOVE

It was not many days before Castleton was caught up in the activities of the colony.

"Castleton, you will stay, will you not? This can be your home, here, with me."

As the aging John Harper looked imploringly at his nephew, Castleton was pleased that he was wanted. "Yes, Uncle, I will stay on one condition. You must allow me to work my way in the fields."

"Agreed!" the old man replied. "However, for your labor you shall receive a wage. You shall share in the earnings of the colony. Such is only right."

"But also, Uncle. That I cannot do. I must pay for my food and lodging by laboring for you and the others. I insist."

"I insist too, young man. It is settled. You must have wages for your labor. You must." Whereupon the old gentleman winked. "Besides you might want to raise a family yourself some day and settle down. You will need some earnings to do so! Now then, now that that is settled, here is what you will be assigned to do." He proceeded to give the young Castleton a list of his responsibilities. Castleton was fairly well staggered at the number of duties he would have to assume. However, when he analyzed them, he realized that the wise, old man had assigned him tasks that would hold him in good stead in the future. He was going to teach his young nephew how to start and run a colony.

Days, months and years passed. Schooled in the art of cultivation, Castleton Harper became the right hand man of his Uncle John. It troubled the young man that his mentor was becoming more and more feeble. In contrast Castleton was older, more robust, and very much a man in his own right. Heavy duties strengthened his muscles. Increasing responsibility strengthened his brain. On a beautiful fall day a wagon train rode into Oxford. Castleton, as well as others, stopped their chores as they watched with interest the coming of a new family to their midst. They looked worn from their long journey. But they beamed with happiness as they approached the settlement. Alongside a covered wagon rode a mustached man astride a sorrel horse with a musket hanging from his side. In the rear was a small boy on a small dapple pony. The wagon was pulled by two, sweat-covered mules. On the seat with the reins in hand sat a middle-aged woman with blondish hair. And to her side sat a lovely, young girl who appeared to be about sixteen years of age. The whole village abandoned their chores to greet the newcomers.

"Hello," shouted the man astride the horse. "Name's Quincy. Henry Quincy. This here's my missus, Mary, my son, Jacob, and daughter, Rebecca. This Oxford? That's what we are looking for."

"Come, come, come in," echoed from all directions. Soon the whole village was preparing a celebration feast to welcome the new family. Castleton busied himself preparing fires for special baking and cooking, carrying cords of wood and fresh water from the spring for the village cooks, generally doing busy work. All the while he was trying to get glimpses of Rebecca. He had never seen such a beautiful woman in all of his life. When his eyes fell upon her the first time, he was smitten. After a time he realized that he was trying to show off to the young girl. She did not frown at his flirting but smiled and blushed in his direction whenever their eyes met.

The Quincys established themselves without difficulty in the village. In time the village men had a cabin erected for them.

Castleton helped in the construction. Rebecca often stood and watched. The young couple became friends. They would take long walks into the fields. "Rebecca, don't go beyond the clearing, you hear?" Words such as this would linger in the air as she and Castleton would take to the trail on one of their long walks. "No, Mother, Cass and I are going down as far as the spring." The twosome spent hours talking about everything.

"Rebecca, do you like the Indians as much as I do? You know, they saved my life."

"Oh, Cass, I do. It seems such a shame the way some of the settlers mistreat them. It is no wonder that they fight against us. We are taking away their life."

"I shall always be their friend, no matter what happens."

"Rebecca, do you ever think of going somewhere and starting a place all of your own?"

"Where, Cass? Where?"

"Oh, I don't know. Some place far away. Some place where a plantation could be built, a home of your own?"

"Well, Cass. I don't reckon so. But it would be fun, wouldn't it. Especially if you could go with someone that you love, and build it together."

This time it was Castleton's turn to blush. "Oh, 'Becca, can I call you 'Becca?" She smiled. "I know we haven't known each other long enough, but some day, perhaps you, and **I,** perhaps the two of us could go away together. Perhaps the two of us could settle our own land?"

"Are you asking me something, Cass?"

" 'Becca, will you marry me?" He stammered out his words, grabbed her hand and kissed it with a long-lingering kiss.

"Oh, Cass. I can't. I just can't. There's Ma and Pa. What would they do without me? Who would look after Jacob? Who would look after them? Oh, Cass, I can't." She stood up and began running back up the trail to her cabin.

The time that followed was a nightmare to Cass. He went about his work with little or no enthusiasm. He decided all the light in his life had been extinguished. Several days after

Rebecca rejected his proposal, Castleton met his cousin, Robert, on the trail.

"Coming to my wedding on Saturday, Cass?" Robert asked.

"Yes, yes, of course. I will be there."

"Rachel is getting a wee bit scared of the whole thing, it appears to me."

"Well, Robert, I don't know anything about weddings. Much less about women." He grimaced as he remembered his own injured feelings after proposing to Rebecca.

"Gosh, Cass, I don't know if it is this marriage business or if Rachel is worried about the trip." Whereupon Robert began to tell Castleton about his plans for taking his bride to his newly purchased holdings at the fork of the Potomac and Shenandoah Rivers.*

His cousin had a lot to tell him, and so the two young men settled down to talk at the edge of a long field of corn.

"Like to plant me some of that tall corn up above the river," Robert shared.

"Where is this place exactly?"

"It's at the meeting place of these two big rivers, Cass. It'll be a perfect place to operate some kind of a ferry over the water. Folks are having a terrible time crossing the rivers there with all of the snags and boulders. Foam just spills over them. The course'd be tricky, but I think there is a safe way across, especially if you know where it is." He continued. "Folks I bought it from call it 'the Hole' because right above it is a very high point of land, from which you can look over mountains a hundred miles away.* It's spectacular, Cass. Spectacular!"

"How'd you happen on this place, Robert?"

"I was going to Opequon near Winchester to help a group of Quakers in building their meeting house, * when I happened on it. For months now I have been working on getting the deed for it for two hundred acres. It was part of a large tract of land given a man by the name of Lord Fairfax by the King Charles. Do you know who I mean?"

Castleton nodded.

"After I saw it, I knew I had to have it. 'Course I had to convince Rachel first, to go with me. That was a hard job to do." He laughed. "But she finally agreed to come with me. We set the wedding date as soon as I got the deed to the land." He stopped talking to Castleton and talked as if to himself. "That will be hard on my Rachel, going so far, by land of course. I could never take her by canoe. That would be too dangerous and hard on Rachel.

"How far is it, Robert?"

"I'm not sure of the distance, but I think it will take us a month or so to arrive."

"Are the Indians friendly?"

"As far as I know, they are. As far as I know."

"God bless you, Robert. God bless you and Rachel." Robert got up to leave, and the story of his impending adventure was over. The flame and desire to do likewise had been implanted deeply within Castleton's heart.

The wedding of Rachel and Robert Harper was a gala affair. It was sad, however, when the couple departed, bound for the wilderness. Two other men and their wives volunteered to accompany them on the perilous journey. As they rode away, the villagers had the feeling that they would never see the couple again.

One year later, a lone rider came into the village. He had come a long way and was en route to Philadelphia. He had a letter from Robert and his bride. That evening the entire village gathered as John read the letter to them:

"'Dear Friends of Oxford:

Thou wouldst be pleased to know Rachel and thy humble servant are firmly established in God's wilderness on the shores of the two mighty rivers. The experiences we have endured have been staggering. But God has provided our deliverance on many occasions. The Indians have been friendly and helpful, thank God. However, we have been at the mercies of the weather more than once. We had been fetching travelers across the river for some time when heavy rains did cause the rivers to swell beyond proportions. Our log cabin which we had built on the shore was washed away, together with most of our supplies. We guess it was not too bad.

For the Indians tell us of the 'pumpkin flood' when pumpkins brought from Indian gardens upstream filled the river and banks of the river. That must have been terrible and frightening.. Thank God we were saved from such as this. In spite of adverse weather, the Almighty has blessed us. Traffic over the river has increased markedly. Thy humble servant has constructed a mill for grinding the corn we have been able with God's grace to grow. It is on what we have called, Virginius Island. Rachel and thy humble servant are now constructing a stone tavern to house us and the weary travelers that happen by. It is to be much further from the river and on a high place so that we might avoid the flooding and beastly crop of mosquitoes. Rachel seemingly is well. She has not yet been blessed with children, but we are hopeful God will see fit to send us a son. But in His time. Thy prayers for our safe-keeping are coveted. Signed, Robert.

Included with it was a note from Rachel:

"It is with great inadequacy thy servant dost pen these letters. My prayers lie with my mother and father. I pray that good health remain with them. The journey to this our home on the river was well, however certain fears during the journey shall always remain with this thy humble servant. Crossing the rivers didst cause thy sister to have a mighty flight. Only with one of the men and a canoe to carry me to the other side didst thy sister make the first great water crossing. The canoe was very small and shallow, so that it seemed ready to take in water, which greatly terrified this frightened soul. But with my eyes steady, and my hands fast on each side, and not moving my tongue, the tiny canoe soon was on the shore which saluted my feet, and put thy servant's pain away. Fearful thy servant became when this same soul spoke of a bad river to come. He said the river was so fierce a horse could sometimes hardly stem it. It seemed a short venture of time when thy servants entered a thicket of trees and shrubs. I didst perceive my horse going on a descent of a hill which as we came nearer to the bottom was totally dark with trees surrounding it. But your sister knew by the going of the horse we had entered the water, which my guide told me was the hazardous river he had told me of. The

Almighty did prevail. For he, riding close by my side, bid me not to fear, we should be over immediately. Thy servant rallied all of her courage, knowing that either she venture the fate of drowning, or be left alone in the wood. The reins were loosened after thy servant's guide did instruct, and soon we got safe to the other side. The fearsomeness of this traversing shalt and whilst be forever ingrained in this mind of thy humble servant Signed, Rachel. "

After these letters were read to the villagers, everyone was quiet, each caught up in his or her own thoughts. Finally one spoke. "All thy humble servants, thank God, the Almighty, for the deliverance of Robert and Rachel. Amen." With that the group dispersed.

NUPTIALS AND THE FUTURE

Even though time passed, Castleton did not lose his love for Rebecca. It grew. Frequently the twosome would take long walks together as they did before the fateful day that Castleton proposed. Most of the time their conversation was light. The young man did not propose again. It would have hurt too much for him to be turned down another time if he made a second proposal of marriage. Finally one day, Rebecca, herself, brought the subject matter up.

"Cass, my pa and ma have been talking about moving on. They like it here, but they think there is more to be gained by moving to another place. I don't know what to do. I can't leave you!" She suddenly burst into tears. "If you still want me, Cass, I will marry you, I will!" She cried even harder.

Castleton could not believe what he was hearing. With his arms outstretched he gathered her up and kissed the tears from her cheeks. "Rebecca Quincy, will you marry me? Please say that you will. I must hear it again!"

"Oh, Cass. Yes, I will marry you. And you can go with us, Cass, with me, Pa, Ma and Jacob. We will be a nice, big family. Will you go, Cass? We can find another place, one all of our own."

Castleton gently took her shoulders and held her so that he could look fully into her eyes. "Rebecca, I want you to be my wife. I promise that we will go. Just when, or where I do not know. But as your future husband, I must buy a land-holding somewhere so that we can settle down and raise a family. I will speak to your father. He and I will decide just where we will go. The answer is yes, I will go. But I beg you to allow me the honor of deciding where it shall be. Will you?"

"My dearest, Cass. The answer is yes. Speak to Pa. I am sure he will agree. It is only right that you men-folks decide the direction of our future."

With light steps and light hearts the happy couple returned to the village, and after asking Rebecca's parents for her hand, Castleton took his bride-to-be to his Uncle John for his blessings on the forthcoming nuptials. The old man beamed with pleasure and delight. "Thy humble servant often thought of asking thee, dearest nephew, why thou didst not ask for this young lady's hand. May God bless thee and thy bride richly with a long life and many, many children. He suddenly appeared weak and very weary. "Now children, if thou wouldst excuse thy humble servant, thy humble servant wouldst lie down and rest.

After the couple left John Harper, Castleton said to Rebecca, "My dear uncle is getting so very old, so very old. My concern for him is very deep. But come, we have a lot of preparing and talking to do!

CASTLETON AND REBECCA MARRY

Dressed in a white cape that hung loosely on her shoulders, a gathered white bodice sewn on to a long, full-gathered, white skirt, the young bride, Rebecca Quincy, walked down the aisle of the meeting house of the Quakers in Oxford, Pennsylvania to become the wife of Castleton Harper. As in the instance of Robert and Rachel Harper's wedding, it was a festive affair for the entire village. As was the custom, the newlyweds moved in with Rebecca's family. Castleton did not mind, in fact he had grown very fond of his father-in-law. The two of them enjoyed talking together and spent many hours and nights discussing their intended migration from Oxford. Castleton had not broached the possibility of such to his elderly uncle.

One day the old gentleman called Castleton to his bedside. He had become much too feeble to be up and about the village. The sight of him bedridden tore at the young man's heart. It was almost too much to bear.

"Good morning, Uncle John, I trust you rested well last evening, and that you are feeling somewhat fit today. "

"Sit down, nephew. Sit down. Thy humble servant is feeling rather poorly, but the Almighty sustains. Thy humble servant is ready for the will of the Heavenly Father. But enough of talk about thy humble servant. Thee and thy future are the concern at this point of thy humble servant." He gave a big smile. "God didst bless thee richly with Rebecca. What a comely, young woman! Thank God for His gift of her to thee!" Castleton smiled and nodded. "Castleton, young nephew, thou must leave Oxford soon and find thy own way. To stay in Oxford forever is not for thee nor thy young bride!" Castleton's mouth stood agape. He was amazed to hear these words coming from the mouth of his beloved uncle. His uncle continued.

"As young as thou art, thou must make thine own way, find thine own place, fill thine own dreams! Thou shouldst not be forced to be burdened by the future of what the Almighty has seen fit to bestow upon thy humble servant here in Oxford. "

"But Uncle John, I like it here; I..."

"Hush, Castleton. Thou must hear thy humble servant out. Thy humble servant wishes to give thee and thy lovely wife a gift for thy wedding, a gift of land." He paused as if he had a sudden spurt of pain shoot through his side and back.

"Uncle, please. This is too much. You must rest."

"Nonsense. Thy humble servant's final resting place is soon to be. There will be much time for rest, much time." He rear-ranged himself in the bed, and continued.

"Castleton, thy humble servant's friend, William Penn, in addition to the land in and around Oxford also bequeathed thy humble servant a gift of fifty acres in what is now called Virginia.

The land is in mid-Virginia. Thee and thy bride must go there. Thy humble servant has the paper here for thee and thy wife. Here is the deed to this land. Thy humble servant begs thee and thine to go!" With a shaking, withered hand he gave Castleton a yellowed sheet of paper. "Thy humble servant has transferred thy name to the title. Wilt thou and thy wife go in place of thy humble servant? Thou knowest thy humble servant will soon be meeting the Eternal Father. My prayers will go with thee." He laid back down on the bed and soon closed his eyes. He appeared to be asleep, once again.

In a daze the young Castleton stood aside his beloved uncle's bed. He was too stunned to reply. He was unable to speak, much less offer a protest. Quietly he left his uncle's room, and hastened home to his cabin.

That night he gathered Rebecca, her mother and father, and brother, Jacob, around the fire and told them of the gift that had been given him by his beneficent uncle. He unrolled a long roll that he had tucked securely in his waistcoat. He showed the astonished group his gold coin, and the accumulation of money he had saved during his years of apprenticeship with his uncle. He even had the family's coat of arms to show the astonished group. After everything the parchment had been through, it was still in one piece. Castleton's copy of the coat of arms was still intact. Rebecca and all of the family laughed when he told them all they had to act like Harpers, and be fierce, fighting, wild pigs. He and his family had the money, to buy the supplies they would need, steel determination, and courage to leave the comfort and safety of Oxford and head for the wilderness. The Quincy's and the Castleton Harper's would go to Virginia.

THE BEGINNING

There was a lot to do.

"Pa, I didn't realize it would take so much time getting ready to make the trip."

"Aye, Lad," Castleton's father-in-law replied. "The journey will be long. We must be prepared for everything."

"With spring about to come we should not have too much trouble with bad weather. "

"Cass, I don't know that that will be true. Sometimes winter has a way of coming back even though we might think it is over. Too, rain might be a factor. Well, at any rate, regardless of the weather, we certainly must take plenty of supplies. We will be on the trail for a long time."

Castleton thought about that for a moment. He much admired the wisdom of Henry Quincy. "How long will that be?"

"Considering the fact that we will be going over two hundred miles, Son, we probably will be on the trail for over three months, at least."

"I can't believe it!"

"If it takes less time, fine. At least we will be ready for all eventualities."

The conversation between the two ended as each one hurried about getting things together. The extent of the caravan when it eventually left Oxford was two mules pulling a covered wagon, two riding horses, with a smaller mount for the younger boy, Jacob. The party consisted of the young Jacob, Castleton, and his father-in-law, Henry, Rebecca, and Rebecca's mother, Mary.

The newlyweds were a-twitter with thoughts of the journey and a new life in a far away place. The ailing John Harper, who was so anxious for the young couple to start on their own exploration in Virginia, was quiet, reflective, and full of much-needed advice for the young pair. It appeared as though spring was on its way.

"Pa," Castleton addressing his father-in-law said as the family gathered around the fireplace one night in early spring. " 'pears to me that the days are getting milder. Perhaps we should soon be on our way. What do you think?"

"Well, Son, I thought the same thing this morning. We certainly have everything ready and packed up. I see no reason that the day after tomorrow we shouldn't be pushing on."

Whereupon Castleton stood up. "Well, family, it looks like we men-folks agree on the matter." He looked at Rebecca and his mother-in-law with a questioning and half-pleading look. "Can you ladies be ready to leave the day after tomorrow?"

Mary and Rebecca both gave a rather wane, half-hearted smile. Looking at each other, the two of them sighed as one but each seemed to give the other courage. Together, but in her own way, each answered, "We will be ready." Castleton could not sleep that night. Rebecca was equally restless. It was like every other night they had known since their marriage. It was quiet and restful, with the night creatures chirping and the frogs croaking signals to each other. The young couple laid side by side in the darkness of the stout cabin in their village home. How different it would be as they would bed down on the trail in the wilderness, night after night! The young man held her close and whispered, "Rebecca, my dearest one, this will be very hard on you and your mother. Do you really think you want to go? Are you up to it?"

She shivered as she moved closer to her protector. "Cass, I am afraid. Yes, I am. But with God's providence we will be all right; I pray so." She was quiet a little longer and then murmured in his ear. "Cass, I am with child. We will have a baby, my love. My calculations are that we will have a child in five months or so."

Castleton Harper was thunderstruck. He had never thought much about becoming a father. He knew he loved Rebecca, but to have a child! Such was beyond his hopes or dreams! To think that he would have a son was a thought that was almost too much for him to comprehend.

"Oh. Rebecca." he held her close. "It will be a boy. I know it will be a son!" Suddenly he bolted upright in the bed. "We cannot go. My son must be born here! Here! Where you can have some help! Where you will be safe! We cannot go! I will not leave!"

"Cass! Hush!" she ordered. "You will awaken the entire family! You know we will go! We will go on! Other women have had their babies in the wilderness! I can too, I must!"

" 'Becca, if anything would happen to you, I..." he never finished.

70

"Castleton Harper, I will not listen to another word. We will leave the day after tomorrow! That is settled. And Cass, please do not tell Ma and Pa about the baby. They would worry too much!"

The young husband held his teen-age wife closely for the rest of the night. He knew that he had married a woman with a rare streak of independence and courage that would stand her in good stead in the days, weeks and months ahead, in the long trek to Albemarle County, Virginia. Rebecca Quincy Harper was a pioneer in the truest sense of the word.

THE TREK

Two days later they left Oxford. Everyone was on hand to bid them a tearful goodbye. When Castleton told his uncle goodbye, he wept. The good, Christian man, soon to go home to be with the Lord, gave him his blessing; the caravan rolled out.

The older man, Henry, was full of optimism. He and his wife, Mary, were in excellent health. Rebecca and Castleton appeared to be likewise, although he had been puzzled by his daughter's recent morning sickness. Their young son had the enthusiasm of his youth. He knew that Jacob would do well. They were laden with supplies for the journey. The air was crisp but smelled of a soon-to-be, an ever-welcomed springtime. And in his pocket he held the directions, which had been painstakingly mapped after weeks and months of consulting pilgrims that had passed through Oxford, either on their ways going to Philadelphia or else toward the new settlements of Virginia. He was excited about the future. He had been told that new settlements were cropping up all over the new territory, which had recently been opened up by the British. It was a vast land area with unlimited opportunities and prosperity. The last trader through Oxford, that he had spoken to, told him that upwards of thirty thousand settlers had already migrated to the territory. He was thankful that his young, son-in-law already had his deed in hand to the fifty acres in Albemarle County. It would be a travesty to journey so far and have no land left to claim.

As Henry and the others rode away from Oxford, he began to sing lustily. "I am bound for the "promised land, I am bound for... " He noticed several of the Quakers left behind frowning. Singing was frowned upon by most of the practicing Quakers in the colony. Being stolid, quiet, and non-communicative was the norm. He was thankful that he could talk to young Cass, and that young Cass would talk to him. He had discovered that although young Castleton deeply believed in the Almighty, he did not practice Quakerism in the strictest sense of the word.

"I'm a'rollin', I'm a'rollin', I'm a'rollin' through an unfriendly land, I'm a'rollin', I'm a'rollin', through an unfriendly land." His singing echoed through the trees. Castleton, Rebecca, Mary, and Jacob loved it, and soon they all joined in.

The group had been on the trail for four hours. They stopped for a short rest and a small bite of food. Rumbling was heard in the distance.

"It sounds like we are in for some stormy weather, family," the older Harper remarked. "Jacob, tie the sides of the wagon tightly so water does not get in, and we'd best be on the road so we can find a good place to camp before dark. "

They had not gone far when the bottom of the sky fell out. Rain poured on the travelers in sheets. Wind blew. The mules kept up their steady plodding even though the path became more and more difficult to traverse. Time and again Castleton had to take his whip and gig the animals into moving forward. The trail was slippery and full of crevasses and holes. "Can't stop here," Henry shouted above the wind and the rain. "Giddap!" He whipped the mules' slippery hindquarters. They pulled the wagon steadily forward. Finally the group could take no more. Exhausted to the point of passing out, they stopped in a cluster of thick, oak trees. The leaves were just beginning to sprout on the giant trees that spread above their heads.

"Won't we get struck by lightening here, Pa?" questioned the worn-out Castleton.

" 'Pears as though the thunder and lightening has moved out of the area. I think we'll be okay here, Son. 'Sides, we'll stay drier under the trees. "

The rain continued. The wet and weary group had great difficulty starting a blaze so that they could cook some of their sparse victuals for their supper. But finally Henry was able to coax a fire to blaze. They ate, and in a nearby creek that was roaring because of the excess rainfall, they washed the old, pewter pans that the ladies had used for cooking. Henry jested, "You ladies be careful you don't fall in that creek and get a might nigh wet." Whereupon he guffawed. Rebecca and Mary gave him a hateful glance and went about their chores of cleaning up after the meal.

Darkness settled in with its impenetrable blackness, and the group crawled into small, makeshift tents to bed down for the night. As Rebecca slept, Castleton didn't know if the moisture coming down her face was from the rain or from tears. Worn and bedraggled, he decided he did not want to know and soon fell into an unconscious sleep.

The next day was not any better. The rain persisted. The weary travelers strained and dragged themselves along the trail that by this time was almost impassable. Trees that had been felled by the wind time after time obstructed their paths. The two men had to chop and cut their way through, and then pressure the stubborn mules to pull the wagon forward. It was almost an impossible task. The rain made the day grey, almost dark, and chilly. The two women fought off the desire to stop in their tracks and demand that they return to their nice comfortable cabin in Oxford. Resolutely, however, they pushed on. Jacob was the one who appeared to enjoy the rain and the inconvenience, more than any. To him, it was all a great adventure. He trotted back and forth of the caravan with his small pony, singing and laughing as the rain pelted over his face and down his back. "We are bound for the promised land... we are bound for... "

The rain continued coming down in torrents for four days. They had gone only fifteen miles. As they reconnoitered, Henry informed Castleton that they would soon be getting to their first major river crossing, the river called the Susquehanna by the Indians. He also did not fail to tell his young charge that crossing the great river would be a real challenge.

As the wagon approached the wide body of water, the wheels of the wagon seemed to become more and more embedded in great areas of water. "Looks like the river has gone over its banks, Cass," his father-in-law shouted. "If we keep moving, we won't get stuck; the main stream is just up ahead." Then the group saw the river.

It was wide, far over its shores. The water was muddy and swift. Swirling eddies of the rough, rapid current pulled the river southward toward the Chesapeake Bay.

Castleton rode up to his father-in-law. "Pa, it's a cinch we can't stop here. We'll have to risk going across. I don't know where that will be though. The river looks like we can't cross it anywhere!"

"Back about a mile, Son, was a spot of dry land not under water. I think the best thing to do is go back there and build some kind of a raft so that we can float across the river." He pulled out his map. "Look here, Cass." He showed something on the map to Castleton. "If we get on the river here, we can float down about ten miles. Then, according to the map, there's a big spit of land that comes out where we can pull up and get back on another trail. Seems that is the way most folks have been going." As he spoke the rain seemed to stop miraculously. He looked up, "Thank God it 'pears to be faring up. If the weather breaks, it shouldn't be a problem at all."

Castleton smiled in agreement and once more thanked the Almighty for the wisdom of Rebecca's father. Somehow they managed to turn the wagon around and head back to the clearing that was well above the floodwaters. There they camped as the men folks set about building a raft to take them across the Susquehanna.

THE SUSQUEHANNA

In three days the men had felled enough trees and lashed the logs together to make a suitable raft for the family to cross the great river. The raft was big. With great concern and worry they broke camp and with difficulty succeeded in getting the mules to pull it to the edge of the river. The river roared. The men had to shout to each other to be heard.

"Pa, how in the world are we going to get the mules on the raft?" yelled Castleton.

"When I give the signal, we'll give them a 'Giddap', hit 'em with the whip, and make them pull the wagon up on the raft. It'll work. I've seen it done before. Cass, you take the reins. Ma, you and Rebecca get on the horses until we get the mules on board." The shift was made, and with Castleton, at the reins, Henry shouted a mighty "Gye" and whopped the rear quarters of the ter-rified animals. The mules scurried up on the platform as if possessed. Henry's scheme had worked. It seemed almost mirac-ulous, but it worked. The mules were aboard, the wagon was aboard. All they had left to do was attach two, long, trees to the sides. The slender tree trunks served as oars. They were ready to go. Another order was given by the older man.

"Cass, there is not enough room on the raft for you, Rebecca, and two more horses. We'll split up. You and Rebecca take the two horses up river about a mile or so." He spoke as he looked for-lornly about. "It's a cinch the wagon can't get through all this water that's overflowed. Some of it looks too deep. The horses can wade and get through this mess though." Castleton started to protest. But his father-in-law paid no attention to him. " About a mile up, the map shows that the river narrows off a bit. The two of you can cross it there." He looked at Castleton and with his look demand-ed his obedience. "There's a settlement on the other side about ten miles down. We'll meet you there. You understand?"

Castleton knew arguing would be fruitless. With great reluc-tance he did as he was told. The decision to separate the group, he felt, was a big mistake. He couldn't shake a feeling of doom. But he shrugged if off and thought to himself that he was just a city boy that didn't have much sense, and that his father-in-law was in charge. Without hesitation or debate he turned his horse upward along the flooded shore of the great river. Bidding his in-laws goodbye, he instructed Rebecca to follow. They trotted on in the ankle deep and in some cases waist-deep water. The raft float-ed out into the middle of the river, rounded a bend and was soon lost from their sight.

"Come on, 'Becca. If we hurry, we can get across the river and down to the settlement before they do. 'Sides I'd rather cross the river while the sun is high."

Two miles up from where the raft entered the water, as Henry had prognosticated, the two riders found a narrow channel of the mighty Susquehanna and without much difficulty crossed. "'Becca, if you direct your horse upstream, the current won't take you too far down. Here, I'll hold your reins. Now, just follow me."

Remembering the letter that Rachel had written about her experiences of crossing the rivers when she and Robert migrated to Harper's Ferry, Rebecca was white with fear. She patted her stomach and prayed to the Almighty that He would care for her and her unborn child. Clinging to the mane of her horse, she bravely entered the swift, brown current. Later, she wondered if she had closed her eyes to hide the fearsome view. At any rate, the Lord did prevail, and soon the twosome had crossed to the other side. Almost in a state of delirious happiness that they had made it across, they plodded through the water down the far side of the river, and in five hours saw smoke coming from welcoming fires.

"Cass, it looks as though we are about there. That must be the settlement up ahead. "

"You're right, 'Becca. We'll be there before we know it!"

Soon, they trotted into an opened clearing where several women and a group of men were busy as they stirred food in a large kettle over a roaring fire. Thrilled to see them, Rebecca and Castleton rejoiced at their deliverance from the dangerous river. They looked about, but to their surprise, Henry, Mary and Jacob were not there. They had not arrived. They were nowhere to be found.

Immediately Castleton ran to the riverbank to see if he could see the raft approaching. He watched in vain, but they did not appear. Finally one of the settlers walked up to talk to him. "Name's Jorgensen, Sven Jorgensen." He shook Castleton's hand. "Expecting someone?" Castleton proceeded to explain to him about the raft and about how the party had split up ten miles up on the river. As he spoke, Jorgensen interrupted him. "Did they know about the fork in the river?"

"What fork, sir? What fork?" All of a sudden Castleton started to get sick to his stomach.

"Why, the fork about four miles up. Everybody knows about that. If you go to the right, you'll be okay, but not on that left fork. Them's terrible rapids, and a real waterfall of about ten feet or more. Anybody goin' that way, 'll drown for sure!"

Suddenly the bottom dropped out of Castleton's stomach. The fork, the rapids, the waterfall? What, what? Why didn't his father-in-law know about that? They didn't know! They didn't know! Why? Why?

"Sir," in panic he shouted to the settler, "Sir, do you have a canoe? I must go out and see if I can find them. They're out there somewhere. I know they are!

"Well, Son, it's almost dark, and I don't reckon it's the wise thing to do. But come along, I think I can find you something to ride." They hurried to a cove where a birch-bark canoe was anchored. "Here," Jorgensen said, "Take this. But be careful. It's right nigh dangerous on the river, especially after all the rain wets been having. It's fixin' to get dark. That's bad when you get caught out there. But I reckon you've got about an hour before it does. So hurry, you hear. Hurry!"

Shouting his wish for Jorgensen to tell Rebecca of his whereabouts, Castleton pushed off into the swift stream. The old settler had been right. The current was swift, and it took all of Castleton's powers to keep the canoe upright as he desperately paddled upstream, all the while searching for his loved ones.

Then he saw! In midstream was a small island. And on the island was a twisted, broken, capsized raft. Tied to the raft was the body of Rebecca's mother, Mary. It had been lashed onto the raft with a leather thong. Thirty yards beyond hanging on a tree branch was the body of Henry Quincy. Dead! Drowned! Beaten and destroyed by the river! He couldn't believe! He didn't want to believe. Jacob? Where was Jacob? Frantically he searched. His body was nowhere to be found! Evidently Jacob had been washed downstream by the raging river.

Castleton wanted to scream! He did! He screamed! He shouted at the cursed river! His people, the two that he had adopted as

77

his mother and father, his newly-found brother, Jacob, all had perished! "'No, no!" His agony was indescribable. The wagon carrying all of their supplies had disappeared. The mules, all of their belongings were gone. There was nothing. Desperately he paddled over to the limp bodies of his loved ones "I must, I must take them home. Rebecca. God, what about Rebecca? They must have a Christian burial!" He pulled and strained as he tried to keep the river from sucking the canoe away. At last with tears and racking sobs he managed to haul the bodies into the canoe. Limp with the horror of his discovery, he allowed the current to carry him swiftly back to the settlement. He had no fight left in him, only abject despair. Castleton wanted to die! Right then and there, he wanted to die! But a still voice in his heart made him go on. Rebecca. He had to console her, and provide a life for his unborn son!

BURIAL

Mary and Henry Quincy were laid to rest on the shores of the Susquehanna. A separate plot was prepared for Jacob, although the child's body was never recovered. The settlers, though few in number, stood around the freshly dug graves, as they sang with fear, faith, hope and courage in their souls, "Rock of Ages... cleft for me."

Castleton and Rebecca stood at the head of the graves. Quietly she cried, as she clung desperately to her husband. Rebecca had not been the same since Castleton carried the limp body of her father up the shore, and laid his body at her feet. Sven Jorgensen had carried the lifeless body of her mother. When she saw them, Rebecca had collapsed. Quickly the men carried the distraught woman into one of the small tents and laid her gently on a pallet. Castleton was beside himself. After a moment he was able to speak and tell the villagers that Rebecca was with child. The women rapidly began ministering to his wife. They had to will her back to life. In time Rebecca was once again sitting up, aware of her surroundings. At first Castleton thought she was going to overcome her grief, that her mourning would be temporary. But Rebecca fell into a deep depression. Most of the times she would not speak. She cried to herself constantly. Worse of all, the woman refused to eat. But the women of the settlement, many of whom had endured unspeakable travails themselves, encouraged her. If it had not been for them, Castleton was certain Rebecca would have died. They prayed with her and finally coaxed her into eating. And so after several weeks the color began to return to Rebecca's cheeks. Castleton began to breathe a bit easier about her condition and the fate of their unborn child.

The whole time he worried about his wife, Castleton worried about their future. How would they ever find their way to Albemarle County? The odds against the twosome making the journey by themselves were little or none. He did not know the direction. Only his father-in-law had known. And he was dead. Castleton was not a seasoned veteran of the trail. The perils of the long journey that remained before them were more than he could handle.

He chided himself a lot. "Why, dummy, have you never learned to fire a musket?" He wondered how they would eat, how they would find food, but mostly how they would be able to protect themselves from the hostilities of the trail. His head ached when he thought about the beating he had on the trail coming from Philadelphia. He would never let that happen to Rebecca. He couldn't!

It was a fact, he and Rebecca could not go across Virginia, alone. Besides, they had nothing. Everything they owned had been washed down the river. He finally decided. They would go back and return to Oxford. They had no alternative.

He was glad that he still had his money. More than once Castleton felt his money belt tied securely around his waist. At least, it was intact. Also he found comfort in feeling the Bible in his vest pocket, the Bible that had been his father's. Many hours he whiled away on the shores of the Susquehanna as he read and reread the scripture. Somewhere in that book he knew he would find the strength to go on. More than once he looked for the verses, that would give him and Rebecca both the encouragement they needed to continue the journey. Often he was on his knees on the river's bank. "Help me! God! Help me!"

RESURRECTION

The young Harper couple's zest for conquering the frontier returned when a war chief by the name of Warraghiyagey, so christened by the Mohawks, rode into the settlement. Amazingly enough this individual was a white man.

His Christian name was William Johnson. Astride his large horse, he was a dominating figure. An Anglo-Irishman, Johnson was riding through the camp on his way to the Shenandoah Mountains. His mission was as always to deal with the Indians. Known as one of the few white men the Indians could trust in trade, he had gained a reputation among the Indians of six nations, the Iroquois, the Cayugas, the Mohawks, the Onondagas, the Oneidas, and the Senecas. In return for his friendship the tribesmen had joined forces with the British to repel a group of planned fortifications by the French reaching from Quebec to New Orleans.

As always when strangers rode into the settlement, they were welcomed with open arms. The fabled figure decided to bed down with the settlers and partake of their hospitality while he rested his weary bones. He had been on the trail from North Pennsylvania for seven weeks. He had many tales to tell. Along with the others, Castleton was entranced with him. He found out that the Indian name of Warraghiyagey meant He-Who-Does Much. Castleton couldn't help but ask him about it.

"Well, young man," the trail-man boomed out, "I just like the Indians and their ways. I treat them equal, I know their language, and I sit at their campfires." At that he let out a hearty roar. "I even like their squaws." For that statement, the prim and proper settlers had little response. He wasn't finished. "The Indians are the displaced persons of our lifetime. They have been robbed, pillaged, beaten, and tortured by the white man. It is my business to put a stop to such. They like me for it. The Indians know that I am their friend. Oh yes, I have served a bit in the military. I worked with General Braddock when we defeated the French in upper Pennsylvania and New York." He spoke endlessly about his exploits. "Reckon I will be hitting the hay for a bit. I am a might nigh weary man!" With that he excused himself and the inveterate trader went to find himself a place to sleep.

In the days ahead Castleton had many opportunities to talk to Johnson. It didn't take long for Castleton to develop a high respect for the man. In a short time the two of them became fairly good friends. The young man was telling the trail-man about his own adventure with the Indians on the trail from Philadelphia. "They were the kindest, best people I have ever met. I will never forget them. "

Johnson replied to him. "You know, Cass, the tribe you are talking about is the Seneca tribe. They are members of these six nations that I have been working with for several years. Some of them have come down into Virginia near the Shenandoah Mountains. My aim is to meet up with them again and see if they can help me fortify some positions that we have over there against the French. Good people! Good people!"

This was just one of the many conversations the two men had together. Before long the trader ingratiated himself to many in the small camp. In the past Castleton had been talking to the Jorgensens, and several other families about his desire to keep on the trail until he reached Albemarle County. Could William Johnson be a godsend? Could he lead them away from the river? As they talked more with the Indian general, which they discovered he was, they found out that Johnson was planning to take an almost similar route to the Shenandoahs. With bated breath Castleton and three of the other family heads approached him about the possibility of acting as their guide. Sven Jorgensen was the spokesman:

"Brother Johnson, we have been thinking that maybe, just perhaps, if you be going in the direction of mid-Virginia, you might would guide us through the country, that is since you are on your way to Shenandoah and all. Perhaps it would not be too far out of your way to let us follow you a bit through the country. We are might nigh unfamiliar with the territory, and since you've been there afore, perhaps you could guide us through." He took a big gulp as he grabbed a breath of air.

"How many of ya's planning to go?" the inveterate trader asked.

"'Bout four families, thereabouts. Well, what do you think?"

With that the genial man smiled and said, "It would be my honor to do so. Yes. The answer is yes! "

The four men dispersed in a hurry to their own campsites with a renewed excitement. Now, perhaps they could go, and go forward. Such had been the unspoken dream of many of them for a long, long time. Particularly it had been the dream of one young, Castleton Harper.

He spoke to young Rebecca that night as they nestled by the campfire. "'Becca, what do you think? Can you go? Can you manage with the baby and all?" He tenderly patted her stomach that was beginning to fill with a rapidly developing child.

"Cass, when would we leave? And who would go with us?"

"Soon, 'Becca, soon. And you know what? The Jorgensens have said we could share their supplies and use their wagon some. 'Course, I'd want to pay them some for all of that. Don't know if they'd take money. But I would offer. But 'Becca, would you, do you feel up to it?"

"I think so, Cass, but let me sleep on it. I will let you know in the morning."

The next day, before dawn Rebecca Harper arose. Taking her husband's worn Bible in her hand, she knelt by her bed and gazed at her still sleeping husband.

"Dear God, watch over us and our baby. Dear God, protect us I pray! Amen!"

In the morning with a vestige of the former spark in her eye Rebecca Harper told her husband that she was once again prepared to go forth into the unknown. She was ready. Castleton looked at her with love and amazement at her resiliency. And as he strode to the campsite of his new friend, Warraghiyaey, he hummed a song.

"After all," he reflected. "God has seen fit to provide us with a resurrection!"

ONWARD

There were three wagons, eight mules, and six horses in the procession that left the small settlement not long thereafter. At the head of the expedition rode William Johnson, followed by Castleton and Rebecca on horseback. Following them was the Jorgensen family, Sven on horseback, Sarah and their three children in the wagon. The Stephenson family followed behind them in a wagon, and bringing up the rear was the Andrews family. All told there were nine adults and ten children, plus the guide. At first the Indian trader hesitated as the number wanting to join the cavalcade doubled. But soon he relented. Preparations were made. Early on a Saturday morning in late summer the group departed the shores of the Susquehanna River, bound for the southwest. Ahead the pilgrimage faced a possible distance of one hundred and fifty miles.

Time passed quickly. The travelers were like nomads who journeyed from place to place within well defined territorial limits as determined by their guide. He seemed to focus the distance they would cover according to what he knew to be an adequate water and food supply. At times the pioneers would stay at one place for several days in order to rest, hunt for game when their food supplies were low, and clean up their clothes, and bodies. They'd wash and bathe in the streams. Many times playful shrieks could be heard as they immersed themselves in cold mountain water. At another time a group of the children were playing in one of the streams, when a young Indian galloped up to their startled midst. His face was daubed with paint, and his face was hostile. He dashed into the water and grabbed up one of the terrified girls, threw her on his horseback, and galloped away. The remaining terrified children dashed back to the camp to tell their parents of what had happened. Immediately, Warraghiyagey mounted his horse on his way to rescue the little girl. He had an idea where the Indians had camped. In short order he was by their campfire to negotiate the return of the kidnapped youngster. Soon he returned to the settlers with the young girl in his arms. As he related to the anxious group of wayfaring settlers, the nearby Chickahominy tribe was on a rampage. It was well, he told them, that they leave the area immediately. In the dark of night lit only by the moonlight above, the cavalcade stealthily made their way from the territory of the Chickahominy's. Once again the settlers thanked God that He had seen fit to send them Warraghiyagey.

The season was changing across the face of Virginia. More than once the warm air of late summer had been changed into the portent of a frigid winter. Almost overnight as the travelers traversed anywhere from three to ten miles a day, the vista changed. The green leaves became magnificent in autumn colors. The creeks and small rivers that were forded burst with a new intensity as if in anticipation of the winter's freeze. As they traveled, it appeared to the pilgrims that Virginia's terrain consisted of rolling hills, lush, green valleys, and tumbling streams. Wildlife was profuse. At times, as they rolled through the land, they came upon log cabins with smoke billowing from their chimneys. Usually they were located on the branches of clear water. Settlers were beginning to pour into the area.

William Johnson was privy to the history of the state. "This here state is owned now by the King. You know the English first came to Virginia down by the James River that's pretty far south of here. Only thing is the place was so swampy the settlers all died out from malaria and such. Then the ones that were left were wiped out by the Indians. But Jamestown is still down there. If you go south toward the Carolinas, you probably will meet up with it. The first ones to come into Virginia down there had guts. That's the truth. Real guts!" After he made such a pronouncement, the Indian trader would gallop ahead as if he was not interested in any further conversation.

Another time, "you folks know that Virginia back in the 1600's used to reach from Pennsylvania all the way down into Florida. Well, that ended when Lord Baltimore came charging into what they call Maryland now. But Virginia has always been loyal to the King. King Charles II calls this place, the "Old Dominion." Has a nice ring to it, don't you think?"

Castleton and the others were not aware that the group called the Tidewater planters was beginning to move into the Province of Virginia. He made a mental note to himself that it was now 1747. Since his Uncle John was known as a Tidewater Planter, perhaps he, Castleton, would become known as such. With the gift of his uncle's land perhaps he, too, would some day be a prestigious planter. That would be nice! It was certain that the English were controlling the Indians, particularly with someone like William Johnson in charge. Again, Castleton thought to himself, he was certainly glad that he was on the side of the group friendly with the Indians. Because whenever he saw a strange Indian, he couldn't help but break out in a cold sweat.

The expedition was in its second month when William Johnson startled the whole group with his pronouncement. "My friends, I will be pushing off tomorrow and leaving you. You are almost within spittin' distance of Albemarle County, which is about sixty miles due west. There's no way you can miss it." He looked around with a look of concern and love. "There's no way that I'd leave ya's if I didn't think you could make it by yourselves. But you can. Fact, I'm right nigh tickled with how good ya's done on the trail, particular the women-folks. " He got up to leave the assembled travelers. "Got ta head north for a spell. Seems there's a bunch of tribes gatherin' up. I have ta go up there and see what they're about. My prayers go with you friends. My prayers." He stood up and walked off into the darkened trees where he camped for the night.

In the morning William Johnson and all of his belongings were gone. With a mixed feeling of dread and determination the group headed out. They figured if they made five miles a day, they would soon be in Albemarle County. However, it seemed like overnight winter bore down on the travelers. The once green hills, browned by the cold, frosty air, loomed as giant mountains rather than sloping hills to the caravan. Snow began to fall. At first there was only a light dusting. But before too long, heavy snow began to fall and cover the terrain. Winds caused the white powder to blow into deep drifts. The hills became precipitous mountains. It was almost impossible to move the wagons. More than once one of them was stuck in a deep pile of snow. Finally, after days of struggling, the pioneers could go no farther. The cold became unbearable. The women were half frozen; some of the children were ill.

One night, as was its custom, the wagon train pulled closely together. The men made a decision. They would find a shelter in the hills, build some lean-to's, and camp for the winter. There was no recourse. The wagon train was snowbound. It was decided that on the next morning two of them would scout the area to see if they might find some overhanging protection in the hills. Perhaps, they hoped, they would come upon a cave or something of the sort that would protect them from the harsh elements. Castleton was among those that went out for the search. He knew in his heart that if they didn't find shelter they would all freeze to death.

Afterwards around a warm fire deep in the recesses of a cavern in the hills, Castleton recounted. "When I saw this place, I couldn't believe my eyes. Actually I feared that a giant bear or something else would be burrowed inside the cavern. But after searching it, I found nothing. It was a perfect shelter for all of us." He smiled as he saw the smoke from their fire drift lazily up to an opening in the rocks. What a discovery he thought to himself to find a place that was somewhat warm and a place that had ventilation. "God is good, my friends. God is so good. Let us thank the Almighty for our redemption from the cold." The four families huddled around the fire and prayed. Outside the wind blew as a new blizzard swept down. They were thankful that they had constructed a hastily built lean-to for the mules and horses before they had bedded down for the night.

Weeks passed as the group whiled away the hours and days. More than once as they ventured forth into the ice and snow they thanked God that they had found shelter. Actually even though the children might play for short intervals in the snow, the only ones to venture out were the men as they walked the hills in search of the snowshoe rabbit, or the white-tailed deer. Once in a while they happened upon a wild turkey, and then they had a feast. All in all, the group managed to eat fairly well. How did they pass their time in the cave? They told stories and sang songs. More than once, however, the people in the cave became irritated with each other. The proximity of living so closely was bearing on their nerves. Although almost all of the children seemed to improve as soon as they were warm and fed, three weeks after the intense cold had begun, one of the Stephenson's small boys didn't respond. The little fellow breathed his last. With frozen hands and broken hearts the men in the group dug a shallow grave for their first casualty. The tiny, young Stephenson boy had died. The ladies fashioned a small, white pillow of white cloth, and laid the small child on it. They buried the little boy on an undesignated hill in Virginia. The trip was hard, hard, hard!

THE RENEWAL OF SPRINGTIME

It happened seemingly overnight. As rapidly as winter had come, springtime began to burst forth from the hills. The caravan moved out. The pioneers were filled with new hope and optimism. The promise of springtime was unbelievable in everything they saw. Wild mustard graced the hills. Its flower danced and pirouetted with bright, yellow petals. Wild dogwood frosted the sides of the mountains and in the valleys. It looked as though someone had thrown popcorn in the meadows as far as the eye could see. On the hillsides streams of melting snow rushed down into the valleys below. The pioneers were awed by the breathtaking purple plumes of the wild red-bud tree. The herds of deer that grazed on the hillsides in the chill of the mornings would emit puffs of white smoke. But as the day warmed, sunlight would dispatch the frosty air. The creeks tumbled with new life.

Castleton thought, "Oh God, how beautiful!" He and Rebecca dreamed of their own place in the woods, and she thrilled with the idea of planting her own flowers, her own apple trees. "Perhaps next year, Cass, the pink blossom of our own apple tree will be a part of this." It was a happy time of singing, praying, and preparing. Even though the couple became more and more excited as they neared their destination, Castleton looked upon the condition of his wife with renewed concern. With all of the delays both at the settlement, the actual travel-time, and the long weeks spent in the winter cave, Rebecca was getting close to her due date. Castleton knew that if Rebecca delivered on the trail, he would die on the spot. Trying to make her more comfortable became his main goal. She could not ride on horseback any more. All of the bumps of the animal were too much for her heavy body. The Jorgensen's insisted she lie in the back of their wagon. And so as the days went by, Rebecca lay on a pallet as the mules pulled the wagon forward mile, by mile. It was torture on her huge, distended body. All the while Castleton prayed she would not deliver before they were settled in their own place.

ALBEMARLE COUNTY

The wagon train pulled steadily westward. They had gone about seven more miles when they came across a cabin and a makeshift barn set low in a valley. The caravan pulled up. A man, his wife, and several children poured out to meet them. Near the small barn, a corral had been fashioned from trees tied together with thongs. Inside it several horses were chomping on some hay.

After everybody was introduced the ladies gathered for social talk, while the menfolk pulled out their pipes and began talking together. This family's name was Thomas, Sam Thomas. They had claimed their land two years prior. Before too long the men of the train were told that the Thomas farm set on the edge of Albemarle County. They had arrived! The wagon train had made it! They had come to their destination! The worn, pioneer men wanted to whoop and shout with joy! They stifled their desire to run to their wives and break the good news. The women were oblivious to the fact they had arrived in Albemarle. Busy eating, laughing, and talking, particularly about the upcoming birth of the Harpers' first child, they were enjoying the respite of the Thomas' home. Each one of the women dreamed that soon she, too, would have such a place to live.

In a nearby glen by a fast, running stream the settlers camped for the night. When Rebecca and the other women were told they had arrived in Albemarle County, they went crazy with thrill and excitement. "Settle down, 'Becca. I don't want you to carry on so! The way you are running around and talking so fast makes me think that you're going to bring that baby on right here and now! Settle down, Wife. Settle down! " Vainly Castleton tried to make his wife relax and take it easy. But such was impossible. Later that night he told Rebecca what he had learned from Sam Thomas. "'Becca, Sam said I needed to go into the town near here, Charlottesville. It's the capitol of the county, 'Becca. Anyhow, when I get there I should go to the courthouse and have this deed that Uncle John gave us, recorded. As soon as they write it in the books, it is ours. And then I reckon we'll get a few supplies and head out to our place. What do you think?"

Rebecca couldn't contain herself In spite of her tremendous girth she spun around the campfire and squealed. "Oh, Cass. Oh, Cass. I've never been so happy! I've never been so excited! This is the best day of my life!"

THEIR OWN PLACE

The next day Castleton saddled his horse for the ride into Charlottesville. Rebecca stopped him. "Cass, Cass. I must go with you. I must!

"Rebecca, don't be silly. You cannot go now. You cannot. The baby. Think of the baby.

"Nonsense, Cass. The baby will be fine. Either I go with you, Castleton Harper, or I'll find a way to get there by myself!"

With determination, Rebecca breathed fire through her eyes. Realizing that she meant what she said, Castleton eased his horse over to the side of the wagon, and very gently helped his wife on its back. "'Becca, sweet, hang on to me now. You know I hate like anything you doing this! But you hang on, and I'll try to take it real easy."

"Cass, I've got to be with you at an important time like this. You can't leave me here. I'll die not knowing how everything about the land went. I've got to go.

"All right, all right. I've agreed, haven't I?" They started off.

Several of the other women ran to the clearing as they shouted after the couple. "Castleton, Rebecca, come back. Don't' you know that baby will be here right away? Come back!"

The twosome paid no heed. Rebecca clung to the waist of Castleton with her big stomach protruding into his back. They started off for Charlottesville.

Sam Thomas had told Castleton that Charlottesville was six miles away. Gingerly, Castleton guided his horse up and down the hills. The beast seemed to sense that it should proceed with caution. It took its time. They had been on the way about three miles when Rebecca felt her first pain. She shrugged it off as an attack of gas. She was sure that she was not ready to deliver her child. As they trudged along, however, her pains grew steadily worse, and came at more rapid intervals.

"Cass, Cass." Rebecca finally spoke. "I don't think I'm doing so well. The baby. Cass, I think the baby is starting to come."

"Oh, God, Almighty!" wailed Castleton. "What shall I do? What shall I do? 'Becca, hold on now, you hear. Hold on." He gigged the horse so it started into a fast trot. Rebecca let out a shriek.

"Cass, stop! Stop! Get me down, Cass! Now! I can't take any more. Get me down!"

With perspiration running off his forehead and burning his eyes Castleton stopped the horse and gently lifted his wife off the horse and laid her on the ground. "Oh, God Almighty! What shall I do? What shall I do?" Castleton Harper was ready to die.

Between her moans and her shrieks, the valiant, pioneer woman managed to tell her husband what to do. She had witnessed a birthing herself. "God," she prayed through clenched teeth. "Help me. Help me. Help the baby!" In spite of her muttered instructions Castleton could do nothing. He was completely helpless.

Temporarily, however, the terrible pain seemed to subside for a bit. "Do you think you can make it, 'Becca? Town is not too far up the path. I'll get you help."

All of a sudden the pains return and this time in more rapid succession. Between gasps Rebecca mouthed her worse fears to her panic-stricken husband. "No, Cass. No, it's too late. The baby is coming now, soon!" With that she screamed again as she tried to cope with the pains that were almost constant.

Suddenly from behind them came a loud noise of galloping hooves and a clattering wagon. Castleton could not believe his eyes. God had answered his prayer! The Jorgensens wheeled up and quickly came to a stop as their horses plowed up on the dusty trail.

As Sven pulled the horses to a halt, his wife, Sarah, leaped from the seat of the wagon and ran to the side of Rebecca. "Thought this would happen." She looked up at Castleton with a look of 'I-told-you-so.' Clucking all the while, she ordered the men to carry Rebecca to the back of their covered wagon. "Sven, you and Castleton start a fire and boil me up some water. Make it hot! Plenty hot!" With that she started her ministrations to the suffering young girl. She poked her head out of the covered wagon again, and shouted. "Bring me some of that there cord. Quick now, let's move!" As Castleton handed her a piece of cord, she looked at him and scolded. "Now you men folks get yourselves out of here. You're not a bit of good at times like these. Not a bit. Now get!" She huffed a little bit. The men gladly made their way down to the nearby creek.

To the young man time was an eternity. Sven had a hard time getting him to sit down. He walked up and down the shore of the little rivulet for seemingly hours. But before too long he heard what God intended to be the most amazing sound of creation, the cry of a newborn infant. The first child of Rebecca and Castleton Harper had been born. The young father raced up to the wagon and threw open the curtains. "Sarah, the baby, Rebecca, are they all right?"

"Aye, that they are, that they are!" She held up the swaddled form of a tiny newborn. "It's a boy, Cass. A boy!"

Richard Harper*, their first child, had been born on the trail, close to the capitol of Albemarle County, Charlottesville, Virginia.

Three days later the new mother, the tiny baby, and the thankful father rode into Charlottesville. The Jorgensens had insisted that they take Rebecca and the baby all the way to town in their wagon. As soon as they arrived, both Sven and Castleton proceeded to the registrar's office, and in short order both had a written claim to land. Sven Jorgensen was headed for the southwest part of the county. After giving the registrar the paper that his Uncle John had signed, deeding land to his young nephew, Castleton gazed with wonder at the deed that made him the owner of a tract of land that had been the property at one time of his Uncle John. He and his small family were headed to the north fork of the Hardware River, near the mouth of Sowell's Branch. * This was the site of the first Harper claim in Virginia, about eight miles southeast of Charlottesville.

Charlottesville was a small village of approximately ten houses or cabin-like structures. Even though it was small, it was booming, and tourists were filing into the courthouse in droves to file their deeds to all of the surrounding land. When Castleton returned to the Jorgensen wagon with the deed in his hand all properly recorded and verified, he handed the treasured paper to Rebecca to gaze upon with wonder. She in turn handed him the tiny form of his first-born son. And as she looked with love at her husband, she said, "Richard wants his daddy."

Before the couple had left the small village they told their dear friends the Jorgensens, goodbye. It was a heart-rending time. The foursome had been through so much together, their friendship, they knew, would be eternal. Sven said, "Well, Cass, reckon you'll be going over to get you some supplies?"

"You're right Sven. Got to get me a new wagon, buy up a mule, and some supplies. Me and Rebecca and young Richard, here." he laughed. "We've got a lot of work to do."

"Say, Cass. You want my advice?"

"Sure, Sven. Any advice you've got will be appreciated."

"Well, if you take my advice you'll go down the street and hire a couple of those black men to come help you clear your place. You'll need some men. Rebecca won't be able to help you. You might have to buy those men. Ya got any money?" asked his friend.

"Sure do, Sven. Sure do. Reckon you're right. I'll be needing some help. Seems kind of funny to be buying people though, that kind of strikes me the wrong way."

"Well, Cass, look at it this way. If you're nice to these people and give them a good home, they'll appreciate it. Most of them look pretty down and out to me. 'Sides after a time you can give them a little tract of their own so they can have their own place."

"Okay, Sven. I'll take your advice. But I'll make sure that in time they have a place of their own. That's the only way I'll ever agree to hire them."

Before the Harpers left Charlottesville, they had acquired a wagon, a mule, supplies for a month's subsistence, and three black men together with their wives and children. As they all left town together, the young Harpers joined others who were headed out in new directions, for new lives in the brand-new world.

THEIR NEW HOME

Castleton knew that his first order of business was to build a cabin for Rebecca and the baby. He found that the three black men that he had "hired", or so he liked to believe, were willing, industrious, and anxious to please. Neither Castleton nor Rebecca could believe the rich resources that seem to teem from their land. It was evident in the rich, fertile soil.

While the men felled the trees for the cabins, she found time to plant seed. Rebecca prayed for a harvest of corn and beans so that she could provide for their needs. Here and there in the clearing she planted the seeds that she had carried all the way from Oxford, the seeds of apple trees. Every time she put something in the ground she muttered a short prayer to God to bless her crops and give her a fruitful harvest. Before too many weeks had gone by, the men had completed the first log cabin of the compound. Castleton moved his little family in, but not before he made arrangements with the three blacks to begin immediate construction on their cabins as well.

The days were full of joyful work. At night the compound slept soundly, worn by the labors of the day. Rebecca could not believe what a good baby little Richard turned out to be. Often she would sing, "God is so good, God is so good, God is so good, is so good to me!" Sometimes she would think about her ma and pa, and tears would begin to form in her eyes. They would have loved the place so! But whenever she allowed herself the least amount of time for feelings of regret, the baby would cry, or her husband would shout to her from somewhere in the clearing. Frequently he would call her for a little help, but mostly he enjoyed her company and her advice.

On occasion Castleton or some of his helpers would ride into town. At one time he came back full of enthusiasm and grandiose plans. "Yes mam, Rebecca, my love. I am going to be a rich man. Why do you know that a man by the name of Captain Adam Throughgood began life in Virginia as a boy servant? After his indenture time he went back to England and brought back with him a wife, son and thirty eight servants. In seven years time, he had accumulated one hundred and five head rights, and his land reached over 5350 acres. Can you imagine that, my dear wife?"

"Ha, Cass, dear. Are you planning to leave me here and go to England to find a rich wife with a big dowry? If you are, I might have something to say about that!" She poked him in the ribs in fun. "Would you bring back thirty-eight wives, or thirty-eight servants?"

After they laughed a little while, he did become serious. "Some tale, eh what? I heard that in town today. Say, something else I heard. There's a crop that is taking over Virginia. Money is pouring in here for tobacco. If we plant tobacco, we can sell it in lots and soon have enough to buy more land. What do you think?"

"Sounds good to me, Cass."

It was settled. Besides the vegetables they needed for the table, the small family spent most of their time in planting tobacco. "Now," after the job was finished Castleton sighed. "My job is to learn how to harvest the stuff."

He learned, and before long their first harvest had brought them a handsome profit. The farm in Albemarle County was beginning to be productive at last. But not only the farm was productive. Likewise, was Rebecca. Again, she was with child.

94

THE GALLOPING YEARS

Conquering the soil was a tremendous challenge to the new-comers. First timber needed to be cleared, and then winter grain had to be planted. In the fields trees were felled from the stump, cut and burned. Trees were used for palisades, posts, and rails so that the Harpers' mule and horses could not wander. In time the young couple could afford to buy two head of cattle, and another mule. The three slaves and Castleton worked for days extirpating roots and plowing above the stumps so that they could plant tobacco, maize and beets. They even tried to plant several mulberry trees so that they might have a crop of silk, but the trees died before too long, and that endeavor proved fruitless.

Rebecca was pregnant with their second child. Her pregnancy was not uneventful. In her fifth month she developed a fever and ague, which turned into bloody diarrhea. Her black ladies flocked to her rescue. She swallowed pills of cotton, or sugar and salad oil boiled thickly together and made into little balls. She was given wormwood, sage, ground-up marigolds, and crabs' claws boiled into a drink and drunk very warm. Rebecca was sick for many days, but after the doctoring of her black friends, she soon was able to get around once more and tend to her chores. She was convinced that Mary, Polly, and Tilly had saved her life. They were her very best friends. They were by her side again when several months later in 1747 the second child of Rebecca and Castleton was born. Despite the protestations of Castleton, the second son was christened, Castleton, Jr.*

"I declare Ms. Rebecca, you'ns jest made to have babies. If thet ain't the finest lookin' young man I ever did seed." Tilly raved about the fine, stalwart baby. The newest member of the family grew, but not without tangling with his brother, Richard. Everyone in the settlement had a time keeping up with the two, little babies. They demanded someone's constant attention. Once they started to walk, all of the women worried about the babies getting too close to the river. The Hardware River was not very wide, but it was certainly swift enough and deep enough to drown a little child. Besides Mary, Polly and Tilly watching the babies, the children of the three black women watched them also. It was a perfect arrangement for the growing family. Rebecca and Castleton had never been happier. Truly they had one big, happy family.

" 'Becca, as soon as I start getting in some profits from the tobacco, the men and I are going to build you a real house. With all the children coming we are going to need more space. Besides, if I keep selling tobacco, there's a spot or two of land I'm looking at buying; you might just get to be one of those fancy ladies that ride around town in a fancy carriage. Who knows?"

"Castleton Harper, you just stop. Stop it right now. Who says I want to be one of those fancy ladies in town? I'm happy just the way I am right here in our cabin. I won't be needing much more. That's final!"

"Hold on there, 'Becca girl; your husband is going to provide for you in a very big, and nice way. That is my plan, and I'm not about to change it."

"Oh, come on now, Cass. Help me put the boys to bed. You can dream some other time."

But the time started to come around. More livestock was purchased. He hired more black workers, which other whites referred to as slaves. As his farm increased in population, Castleton was able to acquire fifty acres more per head from the English. The acreage he acquired was all properly documented in the courthouse at Charlottesville.

He decided that the time had come to build the manor house that he felt his wife deserved. Besides, Rebecca was expecting their third child. He and his men set about planning and designing the house. The south side of the house would sit facing the river, while the north would reach out with a long lawn that would have a long drive bordered by cherry trees. He and his men decided they would fashion the brick themselves out of clay baked in the farm's kiln. Construction started. Castleton hoped to have the house completed before their next child was born. In the meantime, Charlottesville was in a panic.

One day Castleton galloped up the path to the door of the log cabin. Construction on the big house was about half completed.

" 'Becca, 'Becca!" he shouted. She came running to the door.

"Cass! What's the matter? What's wrong? Are you all right?"

"Yes, I'm fine. But it's the town. 'Becca, the town is being overrun with measles. There's an epidemic! People are dying like flies!"

"Oh, Cass! No! I can't believe it! I don't know anybody that's come down with measles! Why I was just up at the Sowell's yesterday, and they all seemed to be fine."

The Sowells were the Harpers' closest neighbors. They lived farther north on the small creek called, Sowell's Branch.

"Did you take the boys up there with you?"

"Of course, of course I did. They wanted to play with Mikey and Thomas. They always do go with me when I go over there. Why?"

"God Almighty! I hope they were all right, and neither of them was coming down with something." And then as if in afterthought. "How about the workers' children? Are they all well? Is everybody fine?"

"I think so, Cass. I'll check around and ask."

"Well, nobody can go into Charlottesville without my permission until this thing is over, do you understand? Nobody. And that includes all the workers." He hit his horse on its rump, and it started in a fast trot toward the blacks' cabins. "Better get down there and warn them all. God Almighty, I pray that this won't come to us up here. "

As Rebecca retreated into the cabin, she wondered if she should start to worry. But then to herself, "Nonsense. I'm not going to worry about that. I think I had the measles when I was little, and I know Castleton told me he had it then. From what I remember it's just a little rash, and fever for a while, and then it's pretty quick to get over. Pshaw! I've got enough to think about without that. "

The baby in her stomach gave her a series of quick kicks. She talked to it. "Okay, little one, you've made your point. You're right, I've got to get ready for you. It won't be long and you will be joining this crowd."

Two weeks later Richard woke her up in the middle of the night complaining of achiness. His mother felt his forehead. He was burning up with fever. The child slept little or none that night. Rebecca sat by his bedside and tried to console him by putting cool, wet clothes on his forehead. A fortnight after that little Castleton had the same symptoms. She had been a little concerned that the boys had had runny noses, but she dismissed their symptoms as being the forerunner of mild colds. She had not bargained for this.

Quickly she called Polly to the bedsides of her young ones, and she in turn called Mary and Tilly. "Miz Rebecca, I hate to tell ya this, but Mistah Richard and Mistah Cass, they's mighty bad sick. Mighty bad!"

"I know that Polly, but what have they got? What's wrong with them?"

" 'Pears to me, Miz Rebecca, thet these hyar young'un's got the measles. Mighty bad measles!"

With that Rebecca started to cry.

"Now Miz Rebecca, ya go 'n git yoreself some rest fer now. We'll look out after these hyar young'uns fer a bit. Now, git on. Git some rest!"

When Castleton came in from the fields and learned that both of the boys had been stricken with the measles, he was almost frantic with worry. He couldn't help but remember the wagonloads of coffins that were being carried out of Charlottesville. He and Rebecca prayed as never before. "Please, Almighty God, spare our sons! Please!"

Several days later Castleton learned that the Sowell boys had come down with the measles. The youngest, Thomas, had died. And the other was still deathly ill. A pall hung over the Harper household. Castleton refused to go to the field to work. He sat by the bedsides of the boys.

The peak of their fever was reached as the boys broke out in red spots all over their bodies, particularly inside their mouths. The linings of their mouths were blood red and festering. Their eyes became bloodshot red.

The slightest light seemed to bring on excruciating pain. Their faces became puffier as their eyelids swelled shut. There was constant itching in addition to the other terrible symptoms. The distraught parents could do nothing but watch and pray, all the while trying to bath the feverish skins of the boys in an attempt to bring down their temperatures. They developed harsh, unproductive coughs. After seven days the eruptions on their skins appeared to reach their peak, and miraculously their fevers began to come down. Both Rebecca and Castleton began to praise God about the deliverance of their boys. In fact they both had dismissed Mary, Polly, and Tilly to get back to the care of their own families. As yet, the epidemic had not touched the small, black enclave.

Richard seemed to improve rapidly, and soon was up and about, and even though he was weak, the parents were gratified that he had escaped the clutches of death. Such was not the case for Castleton, Jr. The littlest boy had developed a severe cough, and his high temperature returned.

"Cass, isn't there something else we can do? Isn't there a doctor in town, or somebody that can tell us what to do?"

"Rebecca, I'm going in to find out. I think I heard of one doctor in there. I'm sure he's overworked, but maybe he'll come out and check on Castleton. I am in agreement. He is not much better. In fact, Rebecca, I think he is getting worse all the time."

He galloped into town, and this time he came back with help. The doctor came riding up in a black carriage, fancy for its day, but functional enough to get around all of the territory's trails. After he examined the child, he looked up and with sad, sorrowful eyes, said, "Folks, I just don't think there's much we can do for the lad. He's got pneumonia. Bronchial pneumonia. " Rebecca started to sob. Castleton held her tight. "You folks might could try some poultices, hot cloths on his chest. Soak some of them with mustard weed." He gave a deep sigh. "Other than that, folks, there's just not much we can do. 'Course, you need to pray. That's for sure!" Before the doctor had left the premises, he said, "Yessiree! That pneumonia is taking out these measles' cases one after the other. He had no other suggestions. Actually there was no treatment. The Harpers were devastated.

Even though ponderous and pregnant, the distraught mother ran toward the blacks' cabins. "Polly, Mary, Tilly, come! I need you! Come!"

Dropping everything, her three black friends came running to the master's cabin. As they watched the little boy struggle for breath, they shook their heads, and together muttered something. Finally they looked up and spoke to Rebecca. "Now Miz Rebecca, ya go on now and git yourself some rest. Ya look plain turrible. Ya let us 'lone now and we will do whut we kin. We ain't gonna let this hyar young'un die. Nossah! Nossah! Now git out 'chere and let us 'lone."

With that Rebecca hopelessly left the room, and wandered out to sit with her frantic husband. "Cass, our little boy is still with us, and if anybody can make him well, they can.

Pray with me, Cass. Pray with me."

The two of them got down on their knees and holding hands they prayed away the daylight; night settled over cabin.

The black women stayed with little Castleton for three days. On the third day the little boy opened his eyes, sat up in the bed, and asked for something to eat. His fever had broken. For the first time in days he managed a smile.

Again, her three precious friends had saved one of the family. The thankfulness that both Castleton and Rebecca felt was indescribable. Their precious little boy had been delivered from death.

Not long thereafter in 1751 Castleton's and Rebecca's third child was born. She was named Mary after Rebecca's dearest friend. The sainted black woman was pleased.

THE MANOR HOUSE

The boys' health improved, and their first daughter was robust and healthy. Castleton and his men tackled the completion of Rebecca's manor house with renewed interest. It was a challenge, because they had never attempted anything of such size.

One year later Castleton sat on the portico of his manor house and quietly rocked in his chair as he drank in the beauty he had created. From where he sat he could see the river flowing gently by. At that time of the year he frequently saw wild, mallard geese land and float on the water for a time, as they rested in their migration to the warmer south. It was a peaceful sight. Below the portico Rebecca had planted a beautiful garden bound by a spacious walk running east and west from which there was a sudden descent to a plain beneath, from where the lord of the manor could view his livestock grazing. What a lovely pastoral sight! Castleton could not believe that God had blessed him so! Just to feast his eyes on the whole estate, he quickly strode through the hallway that ran through the center of the house to the front door. He flung it wide. He looked out on an avenue of cherry trees that bordered a carriage-way that reached about 2000 feet. Alongside it on each side were graveled walkways for leisurely strolling. With the advent of their new home more and more visitors came either to see them, or the manor. They were friends or curiosity-seekers. He liked to believe they were his friends.

One afternoon he was pleased to see a carriage roll up. In it sat the Andrews' family. The Harpers had not seen them since the days of the trail-trek from the Susquehanna. The women were ecstatic over their reunion and retired to the back of the house where they sat in perfect delight exchanging all the stories of the years that had kept them apart. The Andrews had staked a claim to an area in the southeastern part of Albemarle County. Interestingly enough both the Stephenson family and the Jorgensens lived within a range of five miles from their properties. Rebecca wished that she could live closer to such dear, old friends. But such was not to be. Rebecca was grateful that the new manor house was large enough to offer her visitors a place to stay. The Andrews family spent three nights with the Harpers, and then were on their way. Buck Andrews' last words were, "Got to get back to see about that tobacco that is coming in soon." It appeared that everyone in Virginia was getting wealthy with their tobacco crops. Rebecca shed a few tears after they drove down the carriage-way and out of sight. She didn't realize that often she was lonely, lonely for female companionship that had like-precious interests.

Refusing to dwell on negative thoughts, she quickly brushed them aside and began to take on more of her household duties. It was time for her monthly period. It had not come. She couldn't help but be distressed, tired, and worn. But that night she told her husband, "Cass, dear soon we shall be expecting our fourth child." Even though she was weary from bearing children, she told her husband with joy in her heart. One would never hear a word of complaint from the mouth of Rebecca Harper.

In 1753 Henry Austin was born.* He weighed only five pounds, the smallest of any of her babies up until that time. Of course, the young mother worried. More than once, Mary, Polly and Tilly were her confidantes as she relayed her concern for her small son.

"Miz Rebecca, don't ya tek on so. Thet thar young feller is g'wan be the most biggest one of all. Ya jist wait and seed!" And Ms. Polly was right. As the days, weeks, and years passed Henry seemed to be in a race with his older brothers to get as tall and as husky as the other two.

Needless to say, the status of Castleton Harper, Sr. in the community had risen considerably through the years. He was considered a bulwark of the Charlottesvillian society. He was looked upon with favor by the local judge that was appointed by the queen, and before long was offered the job of deputy sheriff for the county.* He was pleased and honored; his wife, upset. "Castleton Harper, why in the world are you going to try acting like a sheriff? Why that is ridiculous!" She thought a moment. "Let's see, how many years has it been since you learned to shoot a gun?" She looked through him. "Not long, that's for sure! Why Cass, if you went after some terrible person to arrest him, you might get shot! You might die! What would become of me and the children? We can't get along without you!"

"Nonsense, 'Becca, this is more or less of an honorary position. Of course I will carry a musket. But in these parts the sheriff rarely, if ever, is called upon to shoot anybody, or even pull out such. You have a needless worry. Besides," he smiled condescendingly. "I already told them I would take the job!"

"Well!" Rebecca said. She stalked from the room in a huff.

THE DEPUTY SHERIFF OF ALBEMARLE COUNTY

A long time passed. Everything was calm. Even though Castleton was a dashing figure as he rode about the county on a striking, white horse, the deputy sheriff rarely if ever was called upon to assist in quieting any confrontation.

However, all of such ended late one afternoon, as Castleton was riding home from one of his outings about the county. He was nearing Hardware River, and admittedly was anxious to get home. He was bone weary from being on the trail for several days in his rounds. Suddenly, ahead in a clearing hidden amongst some trees, he heard a series of mad, cackling laughs from one, no two, no several men. Each time after he heard the insane laughter, he would hear the sharp crack of a whip. Once, twice. It went on and on.

Cautiously he dropped from his horse and tiptoed up to the clearing. Gazing through the trees, he was appalled at what he saw. Three white men were mercilessly beating two naked Indian braves. Blood was running down their backs. Though the braves did not scream, with every lash of the whip they grimaced in terrible pain. Every time the whip was raised, each time it ripped the backs of the braves, the perpetrators would shriek with more laughter. For a moment Castleton watched in fascination and horror. He could stand no more! He raced into the camp and with musket held high, cocked, ready to shoot the white men, he ordered them to halt.

Outgunned, the three, vicious renegades were overpowered by the deputy sheriff. As he held his weapon on them, he untied the Indians, who quickly assisted him in binding up the terrible threesome.

"Why! How dare you! How dare you do this to these men!" shouted the deputy sheriff. "You are under arrest, by order of the King!"

The threesome proceeded to laugh and whoop their surprise and mortification at being caught in their reprehensible act. One spoke up. "Come on now, sheriff. These here are jest a couple of dirty Injuns. We caught them robbin'! Yeh, robbin'!" The others mimicked their spokesmen. "Come on sheriff, turn us loose and we'll finish 'em up!"

"You will not. You will not! You have disobeyed the King's law. There is no edict for an arrest, much less persecution of the Indians in this county. Where are your horses? Mount up. You are on your way to jail! Now! Let's go!"

Whereupon one of the Indians collapsed in a bloody heap on the trail. The other, who did not appear to be as badly beaten, dropped to the pine needle floor to help his friend. Finally, even though he could not speak, or communicate with the Indian, Castleton succeeded in instructing him to tie the captives even tighter while he attended to the plight of the wounded Indian brave. After Castleton washed his wounds and bathed the beaten Indian's face with cool, spring water, he looked at the victim with amazement. He looked again. It was without question.

"Nokomo! Manamoo! My friends, my friends!"

Although the Indians did not understand his language, they did understand their own names. They looked at Castleton quizzically for an instant. There was a sudden flash of recognition. They smiled and grabbed Castleton with a big bear hug. Castleton had happened upon his two saviors from his days on the trail in Pennsylvania, Indians whom his guide friend had told him were Senecas, Indians who had saved his life. Now it was his turn to help them.

Making certain that his captives were securely tied to a stout tree, Castleton guided his two Indian friends a bit farther to his home on the Hardware. There Rebecca, and her black friends nursed the two Indian braves back to health. Even though they could never communicate because neither Castleton and certainly no one else in his compound could speak their language,

Castleton knew that he had been reunited with two of his brothers-of-the-new-world. And he knew that their friendship would be everlasting.

Deputy Sheriff Harper led the three convicts to the jail in Charlottesville. His only foray with outlaws, as sheriff of the county, was over. Rebecca breathed a sigh of relief.

"Oh, Cass, why do you have to have that job? Can't you let someone else do it?" All of her pleas would not dissuade Castleton Harper. He was deputy sheriff of Albemarle County for many years.*

GIRLS, AND THEN GIRLS

In the years to come Rebecca bore three more children for Castleton, Rebecca* who was of course named after her mother, Jemima, * and Ellenida. * The three older sons would have enjoyed having more brothers, but such was not to be. They tolerated their many sisters. The years were good to Castleton and Rebecca, but they were starting to grow older. Rebecca appeared to be indestructible, but Castleton was convinced that his rheumatism was going to take him out of the world.

Their children were growing up. The farm had become a plantation, and Castleton particularly with Henry was eyeing the purchase of new lands in new counties. His other two sons seemed to be more satisfied with working and increasing production around the manor. But not Henry. He was always eyeing another piece of land. His interest was in other horizons.

As they matured into teenagers, Rebecca became a bit feeble. Her hair had grayed, and her shoulders stooped from years of carrying babies around the house. One Christmas, the gallant mother was no longer able to rise from her bed. Pleurisy and a pain in her chest gripped her body, and she was most comfortable lying perfectly still.

It was not a very happy Christmas.

The girls pleaded with their mother to get well. Her three black women, now also grey, and bent, tended to her around the clock as they tried to get the elderly woman to once again be up and about. Castleton was beside himself with worry. To lose Rebecca would be more than his poor heart could bear. Of that he was convinced.

The family prayed, as they gathered each evening around the fireplace, for their mother's recovery. Rebecca was in her bed most of the winter, but as springtime arrived, she seemed to revive. She took her first haltering steps in months, and soon felt strong enough to sit on the portico in the rocker. "Praise de Lawd! Praise de Lawd!" Tilly raised her hands in thanksgiving. "Ya gw'an make it, Miz Rebecca. Ya's gw'an make it!"

And she did. Soon, she was walking around the house, and after a while even managed to go for a ride in her favorite carriage. She had been bent by the illness, but she, as yet, was not out of the picture. She still had much to do. All four of her girls were in love. It seemed as though their romances had blossomed overnight.

"All I did, Cass, dear, was take to my bed for a few days, and what happens? All of these young swains come rushing around the house. And they are certainly not here to see me! How come you didn't' chase all of them away from our lovely girls?"

" 'Becca, 'pears to me that they're quite nice. Quite nice."

The first to come to Castleton to ask for their daughter, Rebecca's hand was Jeremiah Hamner.* He seemed like a nice young man. He promised to make Rebecca very happy and told the old man that he had his eye on four hundred acres on Cow Branch, or the land bordering James Davis on Biscuit Run.* Castleton had to laugh. He knew exactly the place he was referring to. He and Henry had already purchased it. He also smiled to himself when he thought about telling his budding entrepreneur, Henry, that he was going to have to sell those four hundred acres to his future brother-in-law.*

With many mixed emotions Castleton gave the young man and his future bride his blessing. As he looked at Rebecca, his daughter, he couldn't help but remember the beautiful, fair-haired bride of his past, his Rebecca, how lovely she had been, how

106

young and vivacious. And now he gazed upon her namesake. He gave her a long hug. "God bless you both, my young daughter. God bless you, I pray." The happy couple ran from the room, hand in hand, tittering as they went. After Castleton told his wife, the young bride-to-be's' mother, his Rebecca, the news, she shed a few tears in private and then mustered her smile of love and encouragement to the first of her daughters to marry.

That very same year, Jemima married Edward Lyons,* and Ellenida married Thomas Staples.* They both married well. Castleton was certain that they would be well cared for. Actually, 'Becca, what more can we ask of God, then that someone will come along to care for our daughters? What more can we ask?" It seemed with each marriage, Castleton grew more and more weary. When Jemima rode off down the carriage-way with her husband, Edward Lyons, Castleton felt a degree of satisfaction. Jemima had married the overseer of a 15,000-acre estate owned by Thomas Walker, a gentlemen in St. Anne's Parish in Albemarle, who was a physician, surveyor, explorer, merchant and vestryman.* Walker had been instrumental in laying out the town of Charlottesville into fifty-six, one-half acre lots.* Charlottesville laid in an area of 1000 acres that had been originally owned by a Richard Randolph. There was no doubt in Castleton's mind that Jemima would be well off, and taken care of financially in the future. The couple also appeared to be very much in love.

Ellenida, a much more quiet and reserved girl, married a gentleman by the name of Thomas Staples. Castleton reflected that Ellenida was the type of girl that needed a husband, someone to look after her. She was not able to make decisions easily, but Thomas appeared to be the type of leader that she needed to be in her life. In the years to come Ellenida became the mother of Thomas, Beverly, and Sarah. *

Their firstborn daughter, Mary, was the last to find a husband. Her marriage was to an older man. In fact, Mary was quite old when she married for the first time. She married Reuben White in 1819. *

THE FUTURE OF
REBECCA AND CASTLETON, SR.

A year after her first attack of pleurisy and chest pain, Rebecca Harper collapsed and never regained consciousness. In two days, she was dead.

The entire family gathered for the wake. Carriages lined the carriage-way as the friends of the Castleton Harper's came to pay their respect. Tilly, Mary, and Polly, now quite old themselves, were inconsolable. The entire compound was in a state of disbelief. Nothing could happen to their Miz Rebecca. But it had. She had gone to be with her Eternal Father.

After the funeral all of the children gathered around the old man. Before long the daughters with their husbands had departed their separate ways. Castleton's only grandchild helped him cope some with his loss. The son of Ellenida, Thomas* doted on his grandfather, and his grandfather doted on him. When at last the house was quiet, Castleton, Sr. gathered his sons around him.

"All right, boys." He almost began to cry, but quickly he brushed the tears from his eyes. "I don't know if this is the time or the place, but it's better that I know now. Don't know how much time I have left either." Castleton stopped for a minute, cleared his throat, and proceeded. "Your mother and I always did want to know what plans you boys had for the future. While she was living, she always said she didn't want to pry." He looked up. "Now with her gone, I don't see any reason to waste any more time beating around the bush. What do each of you have in mind to do now that your mother is gone? And what will you do when I leave this world?" He looked at them each one expectantly. "Richard, I'll start with you. What are your plans?" With that the old man settled back in his chair. For a moment his grey head bent low upon his chest. But with effort he straightened up and looked his eldest son in the eye. "Well, come on now. Out with it!"

"Father, I've given it a lot of thought." Richard looked with candor at his father. "1 really have, honestly. 'Matter of fact, I've been wanting to bring this girl in the village to see you. Susan, that is, Susan Ethridge and I have been talking for a long time about getting together. You, know. Getting married and all that stuff." He stopped and looked at his dad.

"Didn't know you were interested in anybody, Richard. But yes, go on. I do recall that you've been seeing a lot of some young lady in Charlottesville." By this time Richard was blushing with embarrassment. "Well, go on. If you should marry this young woman, what will the two of you plan to do in the future, get more land somewhere?"

"No, Father. We would like to stay here on the plantation and help run it. Is that asking too much? Would that be all right with you?" He asked plaintively.

"Richard, let me tell you something. If you stay here with, oh yes, Susan, you would make me the happiest person on earth; by all means stay. The plantation will need direction by someone like yourself I certainly am getting too old to assume the responsibility. Yes, by all means, stay." He smiled. "But let me tell you one thing, Lad. Bring that girl to meet me soon. Soon. Don't know how much longer I'll be around; you know what I mean?"

"Yessir, yessir! Next week, I promise I will bring Susan here."

"You'd better. You'd better."

Now Castleton, since you are carrying my name, I would like to know what you're thinking about doing." As he asked this question, the old father was gripped with a paroxysm of coughing. One of the boys ran to get him a glass of water, which quieted him. After a while the coughing stopped long enough for him to continue. "Well, Castleton. What is it? Don't look at me like that! I'm not dead yet!"

"Yes, Father. Yes. Are you sure you want to talk about this now? Perhaps another time?" asked the younger Castleton.

"Nonsense. I want to know! You might as well tell me now. 'Don't know if there is going to be a tomorrow, anyhow."

"Father," he smiled half in apology and half in jest. "I don't have a bride in mind at this point."

"That's all right, young man. All right! Look before you leap, I always say. When you marry, you marry for an eternity. That's what your mother and I always believed. Now, where were we? Oh, yes. Tomorrow, what will you do in all your tomorrows?"

"I have a great interest in some new crops that I would like to develop on the farm Also, I was thinking about working in some kind of crop rotation, you know, so the land won't go out on us?"

"Smart, Castleton. Smart. I always did say you would make the best farmer of all. If you think you and Richard can get along, it will be fine with me. In fact, I will enjoy having you around. What do you think? Can you get along with your brother, and his wife?"

With that Castleton and Richard put their arms around each other. "Sure, Father. No doubt in our minds, we will make it fine. Won't we Richard?"

"That's for sure, Cass. That's for sure."

The old man answered. "Well, that's settled. Glad to see the two of you think you can make it. This place can do wonders if someone keeps after it, and with the workers you have down yonder to help you, the sky is the limit." He stopped talking as if he was finished for the afternoon. The boys started to leave the room together, as they thought he was too weary to continue. But he stopped them. "Come back here. Still haven't heard from my wander-bug, Henry. All right, Henry. Let me have it. You've got that wanderlust in your eye. You've had it ever since you were little, and it hasn't gone from your face for an instant. You can't fool me, and you never could fool your mother. She always knew you would be wanting to leave some day. Well, what is it? I'm listening."

"Father," Henry began to stammer. "I really, I really don't know, know what to say. Father, I want to leave. Judith and I have been thinking about starting our own place down on that land that you and I bought some time ago in Amherst County.* You know that place about fifty miles from here, due west. You remember?" His father nodded.

110

"So you and Judith have decided to make it a twosome and get married." He paused for a minute as if he was thinking about it. "Well, she's a good woman, smart too, if she takes after her father. That Tom Landrum is a fine fellow, even if he is Irish. He's come a long way since he and his family came to Charlottesville. Good idea, Henry. Good idea. Marry that Judith Landrum.* Marry her, and soon will you? I want to come to the wedding." He chortled to himself and then continued. "Now about that land down in Amherst. I know what you're talking about. I always thought that land would be a good investment for the family and eventually pay us dividends. If you and Judith work it and start a family down there, I would be very pleased. Very pleased, indeed. Yes. That is a good idea. A good idea. Judith and the land. An excellent combination. Go for it, Henry. Go for it "Yessir, thank you sir. Thank you." The three sons started to leave.

"Richard, Castleton, you can go, but I want to talk more with Henry. Go on now, the two of you get out of here. " After the two of them left, the father motioned for Henry to take a seat. "Henry, your mother and I talked a lot about you and your constant dreaming of tomorrow. You know, you remind me a lot of myself, in that I too, always wanted to move on and see what beckons at the next place, over the hill beyond. I've always been like that, you know? Never satisfied. Your mother always said I always wanted a little bit more, just a piece beyond what I already owned. 'Land-crazy' she called it." He smiled sadly. "Well, Son. She was right. She was always right. She knew everything there was to know about me. I shall miss her." He sniffed and sighed.

Henry started to get up to leave. "Wait, Henry. Wait. Look over in the bureau drawer. I have something to give you that your mother and I wanted you to have. Go on, it's wrapped in that velvet packet. Take it out, and bring it over here."

The young man complied.

"Let me have it Henry. "

The old man tenderly unrolled the packet. Inside of it were three items.

"Henry, since you are the adventurer and the wanderer of this family, we want you to have this. Your mother and I do. Here, take it."

The old man handed Henry a worn Bible, a torn scroll, and a solid, gold coin. He explained to his son what they were, his father's Bible, the Harper Coat of Arms, and the gold coin that he had kept and treasured all of his life since he came to the new land.

"Henry, when your mother and I left Oxford and started toward Albemarle, we were convinced that we were bound for the promised land. Your grandfather had such a belief, such a faith..." with that the old man began to weep. Tears ran down his face. "When we came over on the DILIGENCE many years ago, my Father, God rest his soul, knew he was bound for the promised land. And now, Henry. You and Judith, you will be bound for the promised land. Take the scroll. Read it. Maybe it will give you the courage you need. And the coin? Well, take it too. I will have no use for it." He rolled it around in the palm of his hand. "Your Uncle Josiah has the other coin. There were two, you know? I never spent mine, although I was tempted to do so quite a few times. Maybe you can keep it, too, Henry. Maybe you can keep it, and give it to your son, someday."

Henry never knew where his father had stored the gold coin and the Harper coat of arms during the years the old gentleman lived in Albemarle County. As Henry remembered some of the hard times the family had gone through in previous years, he marveled that the gold coin had not been spent years before. He vowed to keep it forever, as his father had. Henry's vow was unspoken, for Castleton could hardly finish his last statement. His breathing was ragged, and massive fatigue set in on the old man. The two of them embraced. Henry knew it was time to go. He gave his Father a tender kiss on his forehead and left the room.

That night after he had retired, Castleton talked a long time to his departed Rebecca.

"'Becca, I think you, God, and I did a pretty good job with all of those children. They are going to do fine, my dear wife, just fine!" He told her many things that he had on his heart before his eyelids started to close. "'Becca, wait up will you? Wait up, 'Becca. I want to go with you." With that his eyelids shut for the last time. Castleton Harper, Sr. had died.

Down in the black enclave through the night could be heard the choral singing of their voices, "I am bound for the promised land, I am bound for the promised land; oh, who will come and go with me, I am bound for the promised land......."

* * * * * * * * * * * * * *

ROSE MARIE HARPER
1031 Sandy Creek Rd.
Fayetteville, Ga. 30214
(770) 964-3900

THE FAMILY OF BYRON F. HARPER, JR., M.D.

CASTLETON HARPER. SR. (b.) c. 1715, England; = REBECCA? (b.) ?
(d.) c. 1785; Albemarle County, Va.   (d.) ?; ?

RICHARD
(b) 1747 (d) ? (m) ?
Children:
Richard
Charles or Charter

CASTLETON. JR.   (b) 1749, (d) 7 Sept. 1819;
(m) Martha Gaines; Children:
Mary Taliferro
    (b) 8 Dec. 1777, Albemarle Co., Va.
    (m) Hiram Nimmo 23, Nov. 1798
Nancy
    (b) 26, Aug. 1778;
    (m) Wm. Old; 23 Dec. 1794
Lindsey Robert Agustus
    (b) 19 Sept. 1778, Albemarle Co.
        St. Ann's Partsh;
    (m) 7 Jan. 1808 Jennie,
        McGill Harris;
    (d) 15, Apr., Abbeville Co., SC
Charlotte Blanche
    (b) 11 Aug. 1781, Albemarle
    (m) Samuel Madison Cole;
    (d) 1819
Sarah (Sally) Royster
    (b) II Nov. 1783, Albemarle Co.
    (m) Samuel Madison Cole, became
        mother of sister's 9 children
Cynthia
    (b) 31, May 1789 (a twin) Albemarle;
    (m) Wm. Harris;
    (d) ?
Holcomb, G.B.
    (b) 31 May 1729 (a twin)
    (m) Martha ?
    (d) ?
Margaret French
    (b) 30 Apr. 1751 near Edingburg, Ga. and
        Harpers Ferry, S.C.;
    (m) Meredith McGee; (d) ?
Elizabeth
    (b) 13m Aug. 1795
    (m) Samuel Hamner, 30 Apr. 1818; (d) ?

MARY

(b) 30 Apr 1751; (d) 11 Apr 1837;
(m) Reuben White, son of Jeremiah and
Mary Martin White; Albemarle Co., Va;
Children:
Patsy
    (b) ? (m) Henry Gaines; (d) ?
Sallie
    (b) ? (m) Daniel Thornton; (d) ?
Nancy
    (b) ? (m) James Colbert; (d) ?
Betsy
    (b) ? (m) Richard Harper; (d) ?
John
    (b) ? (m) Elizabeth Jones (d) ?
    Children:
        Stephen Mercer
        (b) 25, Nov. 1818
        (d) 6 Apr 1918
    Family Migrated from
    Albemarle Co. to south

HENRY AUSTIN. SR.

(b) c. 1753 (d) 7 Sept. 1819 or
1785 7 in Albemade Co., Va.; (m)
JUDITH IANDRUM
(b) ?; Ireland; (d) ?
Children:
Susannah
Henry, Jr.
Edward
William
Pleasant
James Georgia
Mary (Polly)
Joice
Penelope
Elizabeth
George
Another Daughter

SEE PAGE TWO

REBECCA
(b) ?
(m) Jeremiah Hamner
(d) ?

JEMIMA
(b) ?
(m) Edward Lyon
(d) ?

EI.LEN IDA
(b) ?
(m) Thom. Staples
(d) ?

HARPER, HARPUR: (1) Occupational designation for one who made his living by playing the harp at fairs or festivals; at times a musical performer for royalty. English: Henry le Harpur: County Cambridge 1273, Willelmus Harper: County York Poll Tax 1379; Rogerus Harper: same.

HARPER, CASTLETON: (1) Same family traced to Pennsylvania. Castleton Harper: Philadelphia, March 4, 1745 from Ireland assigned to James Stephens, baker, for four years. Could be father of Castleton and his brother Henry of Albemarle County. Settled: North Fork Hardware River and Sowell Branch, Albemarle County, Virginia. Appointed deputy sheriff 1744 under first sheriff of Albemarle County, Joseph Thompson. From records of St. Ann's Vestry, Castleton Harper was a reader from 1773 until December 17, 1775. He participated in many land transactions.

QUAKERS - THE HARPERS (4)

MARRIAGES OF CHILDREN OF CASTLETON: (2)

HARPER, JOHN: (3) Former home: Oxford, England, 1682. Settled southeastern Pennsylvania, near Maryland line; he founded the village, Oxford, Pennsylvania. Founder of Harper's Ferry, West Virginia, a key post in the Revolutionary War, was son, John Harper. Also, one of the sons of John Harper was Josiah Harper, who was the founder of *Harper's Weekly*, a magazine that is still published in New York City. The names and dates of the arrival of this John Harper with his family coincides with what is known about Castleton Harper. "In 1682 three brothers by the name of Harper sailed for America. One settled in New York, from who descended the Harper's Publishers (Josiah). Another with the family started for Virginia but was prevented by high water from crossing the Potomac (John), and settled near Oxford, Pennsylvania. The third settled with his family in Lower Dublin Township near Philadelphia, (Joseph)." John Harper, who settled near Philadelphia, was descended from a Norman French nobleman, that was knighted by Wm. the Conqueror at the Battle of Hastings in 1066.

HARPER, ROBERT: (5) Built Harper's Ferry in 1734. D. 1782. M. _____ no children. Left to Sarah Harper, daughter of his brother, Joseph, the ferry, and part of his farm.

PROPERTY GRANTS TO HARPER'S FERRY: (6)
"Part of 200 acres deeded to Robert Harper in tract of 125 acres, April 25, 1751, by Thomas, Lord Fairfax, Proprietor of 5,200,000 acres given him by a grant from Charles II."

LAST WILL AND TESTAMENT OF ROBERT HARPER: (7)

HENRY HARPER TO JEREMIAH HAMNER: (8)

ROBERT HARPER, VARIOUS AND SUNDRY INFORMA-TION: (9)
"The traditional data of 1682 coincides with a record of a Friend's monthly meeting at Philadelphia; note that John Harper had been transferred from a monthly meeting at Barton, England, which was dated 1 month 3, 1682."

"Apparently the family, like many early Quakers, were fine craftsmen. Robert Harper was a millwright and architect, and states that he built a church for the Protestant Episcopalians at Frankfort. Robert's brother, Joseph, is referred to in early accounts as a skilled cabinetmaker. Since his brother was concerned with publishing rather than Harper's Ferry, it is to Robert and Joseph Harper that our records relate. "

"Robert Harper arrived at the confluence of the Shenandoah and Potomac Rivers in the spring of 1747, en route to Opequon near Winchester, where he had been engaged to build mills and a meeting house for Quakers from Philadelphia. Impressed by the tremendous surge of the rivers, he returned from Winchester to buy the wilderness land at the confluence, and before his death in 1782 had erected a fine mill and begun a stone residence on the rugged hillside. In addition, he chartered the right to run a ferry across the Potomac and prospered in both his ferry and mill operations. "

"Mr. Harper is described as a man of medium height and considerable physical strength. An interesting but undocumented location tradition avers that his sympathies had been Tory, but that becoming convinced of the justice of the colonists' cause, he buried considerable gold on his property to outwit the King's tax collectors."

"At the time of Robert Harper's death in 1782, only three structures existed on his wilderness land, his mill on Virginius Island, a house he had built on the Shenandoah near the mill, and a second more elaborate residence nearing completion on the hillside. The latter was the historic Harper house."

"Harper house begun in 1775, not lived in when Robert Harper died in 1798. Perhaps the death of Rachel Harper (his wife) in interim further delayed it. Robert was childless. The property was left by will to Sarah Ann, daughter of Robert's brother, Joseph of Philadelphia. Sarah Ann married Johannes Wager, Sr., son of Peter Wager, who emigrated from Cleves, Germany to Philadelphia in 1736."

HARPER COAT OF ARMS, CREST, MOTTO: (10) As written. Authority.

---

(1) Adelle Bartlett Harper *Family Lines: A loving Tribute to Our Southern Heritage*

(2) Wulfeck *Marriages of Some Virginia Residents, 1607-1800*

(3) Unknown Author: *Notes*

(4) Ferris & Leach, *Quaker Arrivals, Philadelphia,* 1902, p. 6

(5) Jefferson County, Historical Society Magazine, 1962 *The Robert Harper House: Founder of Harper's Ferry, Including Genes.*

(6) Virginia State Library, Richmond, Virginia: *Fairfax Deed to Harper, April* 12, 1751, *Northern Neck Grants, Book* 5, *p.* 496

(7) Berkeley County Court House, Martinsburg, West Virginia, *Last Will and Testament of Robert Harper*

(8) Albemarle County, Virginia, *Deed Book* 4, Book 4, p. 21, September 2, 1764.

(9) Joseph Barry *Title Unknown*

(10) Burke *General Armory,* 1844 Edition

Various other information gleaned from: James Rodgers, Virginia Rodgers Fall, Marie Freeman Rufus, Arvella Harper Blankenship, O. D. Harper